PLEASURES AND TREASURES

GARDENS

Endpapers:
Vaux-le-Vicomte, a contemporary engraving by Israel Silvestre

GAR

MILES HADFIELD

DENS

WEIDENFELD AND NICOLSON
20 NEW BOND STREET LONDON W.1

Acknowledgments

The author and publishers acknowledge with thanks the permission of the following Museums to reproduce the illustrations specified:
Birmingham Reference Library, 38
Château de Belœil, 45
The City Museum and Art Gallery, Birmingham, 60
The trustees of the National Gallery, London, 56, 117
The National Portrait Gallery, London, 10, 31, 79, 80
The National Trust, Waddesdon Manor, 57
The Directorate of the Schloss Nymphenburg, 61, 62
The Victoria and Albert Museum, 35
The Wernher Collection, Luton Hoo, 53

The photographs were taken by the following photographers:
Peter Coats, 26, 28, 125
A. C. Cooper Ltd, 53, 56, 90, 117, 134
Kerry Dundas, 83
FKV Photo Services Ltd, 4, 5, 6, 16
R. B. Fleming & Co, 9
Gottscho-Schleisner Inc, New York, 98, 99, 112, 113, 116, 130, 131, 132, 133
Miles Hadfield, 58, 76, 77, 85, 86, 87, 88, 108, 109, 110, 111, 115, 120, 121, 129
Edward Hartwig, 122
Istituto Italiano d'Arti Grafiche, Bergamo, 119
W. T. Jones, Hereford, 43, 54, 101, 102
F. R. Logan Ltd, Birmingham, 60
Lady Alexandra Metcalfe, 124
Pucci Photo, 19
Scala, Milan, 12, 24, 25
Edwin Smith, 1, 11, 13, 16, 17, 20, 21, 23, 27, 29, 30, 41, 42, 44, 48, 49, 50, 51, 52, 63, 64, 66, 74, 82, 84, 89, 91, 106, 114
Wim Swaan, 68, 69, 72, 73
The photograph for the jacket was taken by Adam Woolfitt by kind permission of Messrs Crowther, Isleworth

Printed in Italy by Arti Grafiche Matelli, Milan

Contents

CHAPTER ONE

Italy ar

1 The Fountain of the Moors, probably by
Giovanni da Bologna, the centre-piece of
the sixteenth-century garden at the Villa
Lante, near Viterbo

l Beyond

THE PLEASURES OF gardens—what, indeed, we must ask before we embark upon so substantial and yet so transient a matter, what are they and how should we discuss them? First, it seems, we should limit the subject and bring it within ease of comprehension by excluding the pleasures of gardening: no one discoursing on the pleasures of painting gives much space to their creation by the artist. It is the finished work as seen by the observer that counts. The pleasure that Louis XIV, instigator of one of the greatest of gardens, took in them is not, so far as I know, recorded: for him they were scenes for the great fêtes in which *le Roi-Soleil* was himself the centre of display. And of the mind and methods—let alone the feelings—of the genius who undertook them, André Le Nôtre, even less is known. We may turn to Dr Martin Lister, who visited Paris in 1698, for a description of the enjoyment of them: their designer he found a charming and cultured old gentleman, surrounded and absorbed by his curios, medals and pictures but giving no clue to the nature and imagination of the mind that wrought Versailles.

In England, we know little enough of the feelings and pleasures of the creators of the first 'landskips' or *jardins anglais*—Philip Southcote at Woburn Farm, Hamilton at Painshill or Hoare at Stourhead (though Shenstone and his Leasowes is an exception, for he was a writer by profession).

Enjoyment was left to the visitors, the description of the pleasures to Horace Walpole and his kind. In an endeavour

7

2 Nicolas Foucquet, the French Minister of Finance and creator of the magnificent house and garden at Vaux-le-Vicomte, of which he was deprived by Louis XIV

to understand these pleasures we should, I suppose, pay some attention to the views of those who follow the cult of Psyche. But what can they tell us about a form of display that is largely impersonal and aesthetic, designed not from selfish or egocentric motives, but 'to captivate and charm, rather than to rouse alarm'? The creation of gardens, and the ardours of both gardening and enjoying gardens, are all a little unbalanced (unless one is growing vegetables or being paid for it), for they are all concerned with forming or entering into a private microcosm; surely the psychologists must disapprove of this. And to build these substantial fantasies and challenge fate may bring its reward of disaster, albeit that a moment of great pleasure comes first.

The recognition of the genius of Le Nôtre was fortuitously bound up in such an instance of retribution. Nicolas Foucquet, France's Minister of Finance, lavished encouragement, employment and his fortune on the artists of his time. Among them was the promising young Le Nôtre, trained in the theory and practice of design and gardening under the most eminent practitioners to a degree of competence unimaginable today, and touched with a spark which informed his work so that it surpassed that of all others. When Foucquet decided to build a palace and create an estate worthy of his wealth and to display his superb taste, there were no half measures; it must be unequalled in France. At Vaux-le-Vicomte he succeeded in his object. Le Vau was the architect, and Le Nôtre brought himself fame by designing the garden. It was what we should now call the prototype of the French grand manner formal garden which shortly dominated Europe. On 17th August 1661 Foucquet, to celebrate the completion of this masterpiece of all the arts, entertained Louis XIV and his Court. Six thousand guests wandered in the vast pleasure grounds. Corneille, La Fontaine and Perrault were among the guests. The supper cost a hundred and twenty thousand livres; afterwards Le Nôtre's first masterpiece was illuminated, and, somewhere among the spraying, hissing fountains Molière produced a play written specially for the event. Here was display with pride in perfection. 'I shall not dare to invite you to visit me,' said the King smilingly.

Twenty days after the fête Foucquet was arrested for peculation; Vaux-le-Vicomte was empty, dismantled, and those who formed it henceforth served the King. A just reward—a physical rather than a psychological one, it may be said —for one who tried to build himself a world that might take him into the magic of his friend Perrault's fairy land. Yet: Le Nôtre's Vaux-le-Vicomte, reconstructed, lives on, enabling all who visit it to enter into and partake of the pleasures that apparently disappeared with Foucquet's arrest on that 5th of September.

Other escapers into a microcosm of the pleasures of glorious ostentation, or rather their gardens, have not been so fortunate. Oblivion—and suburbia—lies round and upon the garden of Canons made at Edgware by James Brydges, Duke of Chandos, Earl of Caernarvon and Viscount Wilton. This garden, begun in 1713, lives in descriptions only—and Brydges' account books. These show how the world was explored for materials and plants; even the turf was brought from Aleppo, and was mown twice or thrice weekly; perhaps to this day there lie under some suburban villa the bones of his eagles, who drank from specially carved stone troughs.

There was, too, another sad sequel to the making of what James Lees-Milne calls the small paradise of Philip V of Spain around the Palace of La Granja—a masterpiece by Étienne Boutelou in the style of Le Nôtre. The gardens lie in a hollow beneath a snow-tipped mountain. When the elaborate waterworks, with their twenty-six lead fountains 'as good as those of Versailles', threw their jets into the air for the first time, the King sadly commented, ' It has cost me three millions of money to get three minutes entertainment'. Fortunately, posterity has benefited from the in-

3 A contemporary view of Vaux-le-Vicomte by le Coste, illustrating Le Nôtre's ingenious use of levels in creating at Vaux the prototype of Versailles

4 The Villa Pia, in the Vatican gardens, Rome, built for Pope Pius IV in 1560

vestment. Writing in the 1820s, La Gasca said that the gardens were 'considered by many persons to be superior to those of Versailles. What render them most delightful are their fine stately woods of lime, oak, elm, black poplar, aspen, horse-chestnuts and other forest trees. The walks through these are completely shaded during summer, and the air is agreeably cooled by the cascades of water which fall from the elevated summits of the high grounds and by the diversified play of the numerous fountains.'

> There are microcosms of another kind, the
> ... cool retreat
> From all th' immoderate heat
> In which the frantic world does burn and sweat...

So wrote Abraham Cowley, a precursor of those who hope to, and often do, find the pleasures of a garden a healthy escape from the tiresomeness of the everyday world. The followers of this view of gardens include the more illustrious, if rather mad, J. J. Rousseau. It seems, however, that thanks to the assistance of the rich financier de Girardin, his retreat in the garden at Ermenonville was at least as tolerable as his other homes. Cowley, however, found his own little elysium when he achieved it in Chertsey.

Then we must take into account those very real pleasures that are due to the release from some deeply sunken fear. Particularly in gardens are we beset by those almost fundamental states of agoraphobia and claustrophobia. In early times, the cosiness of walled gardens was a necessity, a protection against a world of savage marauders, a partnership with the fortified house or the monastic life. Yet, long after these causes had lost their force, walled and formal gardens continued (the walls were certainly useful for fruit): agoraphobia reigned.

Then, as every student of garden history knows, somewhere about 1720 a stout Yorkshireman, trained as a sign-painter, laughingly jumped the wall, and turned all nature into a garden. Claustrophobia became epidemic. Walls were thrown down, straight avenues fell to the axe, the rigid margins of canals wrenched into meandering curves. The disease crossed the Channel as *le jardin anglais*, and in no time had spread as far as Russia. Soon there was an inevitable reaction; formality returned. And from that time we have had a dichotomy in gardens, the eternal battle between the formal and informal, or agoraphobia and claustrophobia, that provides one of their most powerful and deeply felt pleasures (or displeasures, if one prefers it so). As we are for a moment discussing the more sombre aspects of gardens, in which pain may mingle with pleasure, it is opportune to recall that a number of persons have been of the same opinion as John Evelyn who thought that '*Gardens* were thought enough honorable for those *Funeral* purposes... our most *Blessed Saviour's* was in a Garden: which indeed seems to be the most proper and eligible, as we have already shew'd... The late elegant and accomplish'd *Sir W. Temple*, tho' he laid not his whole *Body* in his *garden*, deposited the better Part of it (his *Heart*) there; and if my *Executors* will gratify me in which I have desir'd, I wish my *Corps* may be *Interr'd* as I have bespoke them.'

Ernst Ludwig, Duke of Gotha—French scholar, mathematician, astronomer, authority, Fellow of the Royal Society and Knight of the Garter—was of the same opinion. It is recorded that on his death in 1804, he forbade in his will all ceremony at his burial, except such as is usual for his lowest subjects. He desired to be buried in his English garden, at the feet of the coffins containing the bodies of his two already deceased children. No speech nor sermon was to be pronounced, and no monument was to be erected over him; but he desired his second son, Prince Frederick, to place a tree upon his grave. To this Prince he bequeathed his English garden, which was to be open, as formerly, to all visitors. The reigning Duchess, with her child in her arms, had, the evening before, strewed flowers round the grave. The midnight hour struck, the body entered the garden,

5 The Villa Pia, which Burckhard described as 'the most perfect retreat imaginable for a midsummer afternoon'

carried by the servants of the late Duke. The walk to the island was laid with black cloth, with the boat that carried it over. The ceremony was only interrupted by the sighs and tears of all present. A contemporary account of the Ducal gardens where this sombre and moving event took place indicates Germanic thoroughness: 'they are remarkable for their fine lawns, and for a ruined castle, which was first built complete, and then ruined *exprés*, by firing cannon against it.'

Before we leave these ultimate and gloomy aspects of gardens, Dr Martin Lister may be quoted again, writing of the garden at Les Diguires: 'In an obscure parterre I saw the tomb of a cat, *viz* a black cat couchant upon a white marble cushion, fringed with gold, and gold tassels hanging at the corners upon a square black marble pedestal. On one of the sides of that marble is writ in letters of gold,

> *Cy gist Menine la plus amiable et la*
> *Plus aimée de toutes les chattes.*

On the other side,

> *Cy gist une chatte, une chatte jolie*
> *Sa maitresse, qui n'aimot rien,*
> *L'aime jusques à la folie*
> *Pour quoy dire! on le voit bien*

This is not the first instance of this kind of folly: I have seen something of it in England, and have read much more in history. If you blame me for transcribing this epitaph, I will submit'.

Important, too, are the spiritual and physical pleasures of material. In the Chinese and Japanese gardens they are (so far as we in the West, who are so little comprehending, can see) closely related to the fundamental elements of stone and water and trees. In Mediterranean gardens, hot from the sun and neighbouring Africa, the playing of fountains, the cascading of water and the shade of trees and arbours—all contrived within a superb architecture—are pre-eminent as sources of pleasure. In the British Isles and North America, the making of woodlands with exotic trees and shrubs has but lately been developed to give us enjoyment of a sophisticated atavism.

Then there are plants. Today, the majority of garden visitors consider them above all the essential part of gardens. Particularly is this so in the countless smaller garden-plots that have been created in prosperous democracies. Never has such a variety been available. Countless American native flowers prosper in Europe, and vice-versa. Within half-a-century the wealth of western China and the lands surrounding it, a flora that deserves for once the use of the adjective fabulous, has been carried to all the temperate parts of the globe. And the plant breeders seem to progress both triumphantly and disastrously (according to one's taste) at a rate increasing by geometric progression in the production of new plants. And finally there is one particular pleasure that we shall mention now and have done with for all, since it is a pleasure that has continued unchanged over many centuries and concerns only a limited class of persons (clergy of all nationalities and denominations are particulary prone to it.) This is that body once known as 'curious' — in the sense of inquisitive — gardeners and now generally as keen plantsmen. They are quite distinct from truly botanical gardeners, having a wider interest touching the aesthetic as well as the botanic qualities of the plants they consider, often discussing with considerable passion, though otherwise they are by nature most placid and courteous persons.

It is from this welter of emotions, sights, sounds, scents and comforts that we have in the following pages tried to select a few pleasures and shape them into a coherent form for, we hope, the entertainment of the reader.

The perplexities of finding a starting-point for this account are, fortunately, largely solved by the limitations of our space. Probably we should (if we were learned enough)

6 Thetis, the mother of Achilles, sits on a hassock of leaves in the Vatican gardens

7 Hadrian's villa at Tivoli. A partial reconstruction of the central ornamental pool, surrounded by statues and colonnades

8 Louis de Caullery's view of Rome in the early seventeenth-century illustrates a garden of the Italian Renaissance, which already foreshadows the type of garden-design elaborated by Le Nôtre

embark on descriptions of the Hesperides, the garden of Alcinous, the hanging gardens of Babylon, the strange Adonis gardens of the Scriptures, or even the garden of Gatholonabes on the isle of Milsterak. We must, however, content ourselves with a solitary mediaeval vision, by Hieronymus Bosch, of the *fons et origo* of our subject—Eden itself [figure 12]. Then for our part we may make a start with the Renaissance gardens of Italy. For one reason, they draw together so many threads of past styles of gardens, and of the botanical and scientific learning incorporated in them. They are the direct heirs of Greece, whence Alexander the Great strode into Asia and brought back great stores of knowledge at the time when Theophrastus, the 'father of botany', was writing. They carry within them the Byzantine traditions and all which that implies. Plants which the Italians cultivated, quite unknown to them, had worked their way over the ancient caravan routes from western China: traditionally Persian in origin, it is only within the last sixty or seventy years that their true provenance has become known. Then there is the underlying theme of the vertical and the horizontal, the great classical orders fundamental to so much architecture. In the Italian garden it is echoed by two trees universally used. The vertical is the narrow erect form of the Mediterranean cypress, famous in legend and literature. The horizontal is the stone pine, with its flat, spreading head that the poets describe as an anchored cloud. (Less reverently, they are known respectively as the closed and open umbrellas). We can gain an impression of early Italian gardens from Louis de Caullery's view of Rome [figure 8]. Here is the substance of Italy that was to be in the first place the starting ground for the Italian style of gardening that was to spread far and wide, even down to the present century, and to form the basis for the French manner that culminated in the magnificence of Le Nôtre. Moreover, it was this Roman landscape that was to become the inspiration of the English landscape garden that developed into the picturesque and later the romantic manners—strange contrasts to the Palladian mansions that they surrounded. To attempt an analysis of the Italian gardens of the Renaissance is beyond our scope: it is a matter for scholars who specialise in it. Many of the most famous gardens have undergone changes and alterations in accordance with fashion. These have modified the intentions of their designers, who planned them integrally with the villas they surround, the outdoor extensions of which they were.

Antiquarians have always delighted in reconstructing the villas described by Pliny the Younger in his correspondence of the first century. His Laurentine villa had, it seemed, a formal plan [figure 9], looking over meadows and the bay of Ostia to the distant villages; this liking for distant views was also shown in his Tuscan garden. The plants grown were those described by Virgil—all of them common in Italian gardens to this day.

We may turn to John Evelyn's description of one of the most celebrated of all gardens, the Villa d'Este, at Tivoli, [figures 10, 11 and 13] in the mid seventeenth century. 'On the right hand, are sixteen vast conchas of marble, jetting out water; in the midst of these stands a *Janus quadrifons*, that cast forth four girandolas, called from the resemblance, the *Fonta di Specchio* (looking-glass). Before the ascent of the Palace is the famous fountain of Leda, and not far from that four sweet and delicious gardens. Descending thence are two pyramids of water, and in a grove of trees near it the fountains of Tethys, Esculapius, Arethusa, Pandora, Pomona, and Flora; then the prancing Pegasus, Bacchus, the grot of Venus, the two colosses of Melicerta and Sibylla Tiburtina, all of exquisite marble, copper, and other suitable adornments. The cupids pouring out water especially most rare, and the urns on which they are placed the ten nymphs. The grots are richly paved with *pietra comessa* shells, coral, etc. Towards *Roma Triumphans* (the mod-

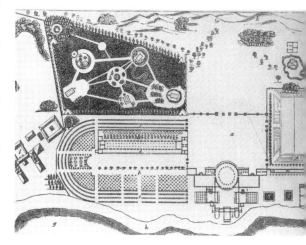

9 A conjectural plan by Robert Castell, 1728, of Pliny the Younger's garden overlooking the Bay of Ostia

15

10 John Evelyn, English naturalist and antiquarian, 1620-1706

11 The Dragon Fountain at the Villa d'Este, Tivoli. The legend is that it was built in a single night in honour of a sudden visit by Pope Gregory XIII

el of Ancient Rome) leads a long and spacious walk, full of fountains, under which is historised the whole Ovidian metamorphoses in rarely sculptured mezzorelievos... In another garden is a noble aviary, the birds artificial and singing until an owl appears, on which they suddenly change their notes. Near this is the fountain of dragons, casting out large streams of water with great noise. In another grotto... is an hydraulic organ, and below this are divers stews and fishponds, and lastly a garden of simples.'

When Evelyn wrote, these gardens, begun by Ippolito d'Este, with the aid of what we should now call a team of specialist experts, were just a century old. Evelyn, in his rambling prose with its well-understood classical allusions, probably got near to the contemporary feeling for its qualities. It is pleasant, therefore, to compare his description with another made at the end of the nineteenth century by 'EVB' (the Hon Mrs Boyle). 'In all Italy—the land of flowers, the garden of the world—there are no gardens more stately, nor any nobler cypress-trees, than at the Villa d'Este of Tivoli. In the spring, by the straight smooth ways under the ilexes and cypresses, all day the golden gloom is made rosy where ever and anon red Judas-trees shower down their bloom. Marble stairs lead up through terraced heights to paved walks under the Palazzo walls. There the air is faint with rich fragrance of the orange-trees. The lofty spires of ancient cypresses reach up above the topmost terrace; far below in the garden, between their dark ranks sparkle the upspringing fountains. Beyond, above the tallest cypresses, rise the brown crumbling walls of the old town, piled up with open *loggie* and arched gates and overshadowing roofs: high over these, great barren hills crowned with ruined fortresses and shattered keeps. To the west rolls out the ocean of the wide Campagna, undulating far away where Rome is lost in the sunset. Dream on, until you sigh with the wondrous sweetness of Rome herself...' Not a word about the water organ! How utterly variable

12 Detail of *The
Garden of Eden*,
by Hieronymus
Bosch, at the
Prado

13 The superimposed fountains of Neptune and the Organ at the Villa d'Este form a single composition of falling sheets of water and jets rising from different levels

are the pleasures obtainable from one and the same garden!

The same lack of unanimity is found with another much written-of garden, Isola Bella in Lake Maggiore [figures 14 and 16].

Of great interest is the account of Lake Maggiore written by Henri Taine a century ago, for he comments also on the classical landscape which through the influence of Claude and others has become incongruously naturalised in England, a country he had visited not long before. He describes also Isola Madre, the rocky islet on which Carlo Borromeo had begun his work but which had later been landscaped and planted with an amazing variety of trees and shrubs. On an April day he wrote, 'If I had my choice of a country-house I would take one here. From above Varese where the road begins to descend, one sees at one's feet a broad plain over which is spread out a series of low hills. The whole expanse is clothed with verdure and with trees, with fields and crops spotted with white and yellow flowers like a velvet Venetian robe, with mulberry-trees and vines, and, farther on, with bouquets of oaks and poplars, and scattered among the hills, with beautiful placid lakes, united and spreading out broadly and glittering like mirrors of steel. It is the freshness of an English landscape among the noble lines of a picture by Claude. The mountains and the sky impart majesty and the superabundant water imparts moisture and grace. The two natures, that of the north and that of the south, here unite in a happy and friendly embrace in order to combine the softness of a grassy park with the grandeurs of an amphitheatre. The lake itself is much more varied than that of Como: it is not encased from one end to the other by naked and abrupt hills; it has rugged mountains but also gentle slopes, the drapery of the forests and a perspective of plains. From Laveno you see its broad, placid surface, scattered with rays and damasked like a cuirass under innumerable scales in a blaze of sunshine traversing the dome of clouds; scarcely does the light breeze

impel a dying undulation against its gravelly shore. Toward the east a path winds half way up the bank among green hedges, blooming fig-trees, spring flowers, and every description of delightful perfume. The great lake opens out tranquil in full view; the swelling sail of a small vessel is seen, also two white hamlets which at this distance seem to be the work of beavers. Mountains bristling with trees descend at long intervals to the water's edge, expanding their pyramids, their misty peaks half lost in the cloudy grayness.

The Villa d'Este and Isola Bella are gardens that have over the centuries impressed so generally and overwhelmingly that they have often been written about by eminent literary persons. The Villa Lante at Bagnaia [figures 1, 17, 18 and 19] has been described by lesser, but perhaps more knowledgeable, writers. Montaigne is the most famous; in 1580 he wrote of it as it then was, not yet completed, as one of the most richly ornamented places he ever saw, adding that waterworks included novelties that surpassed those of Tivoli. Inigo Triggs in his great study of Italian gardens wrote that the means employed in its design were worthy of the minutest examination. The traveller Augustus Hare called it a paradise, and a century or so later Hugh Honour said that it was an ideal garden of the Renaissance. The site, on gently sloping ground, had long been a summer residence and later hunting ground of the Bishops of Viterbo, one of whom built an aqueduct only some nine inches wide that later made possible the construction of the fountains, a surprisingly ingenious example of hydraulics.

In 1566 the present garden and villa were begun by Cardinal Gambara [figure 19]. He did not complete the work, building one only of the twin buildings intended to

15 The Villa Garzoni, Collodi, has one of the most magnificent gardens in Italy, combining the Renaissance and baroque styles. It dates from the mid-seventeenth century

16 Isola Bella, romantic and theatrical, where camellias follow mimosa and azaleas follow camellias, the terraces sheltered by hedges of cypress and yew, decorated with statues and stone urns. This was the place that entranced Turner and Corot, Dumas and Wagner, Bourbons and Buonapartes

17 The 'Quadrato' at the Villa Lante, overlooking the village of Bagnaia. In the centre is the Fountain of the Moors, (illustrated in more detail in figure 1), and around it the elaborate parterre created by Cardinal Gambara about 1570, and now restored to its full beauty by Dr Angelo Cantoni

18 The Villa Lante in the seventeenth century. The house was formed of two separate pavilions, and was conceived as a single composition with its garden, instead of making the garden a mere appendage to the palazzo

form the villa. It is said that St Carlo Borromeo interfered on the grounds of Gambara's extravagance. The work was resumed and the second villa built under Cardinal Peretti di Montalto some ten years later. The heraldic devices of the cardinals who built the place in the form of rebuses on their names (*Gambara* means 'crayfish') are prominent throughout the gardens. The remarkable fountain of the lamps is one feature notable for its originality and beautiful detail. The chain of water is another: the water flows down a narrow series of steps, chain-like in form, to emerge into the fountain of the giants. Villa Lante is by many held to be a perfect example of planning in the Italian manner, the integration of the different parts into a whole, though the work was spread over so many years, being flawless in balance, originality and taste.

The Villa Caprarola and its garden [figures 20, 21, 22 and 42], also not far from Viterbo, was very different in design. It has long been noted for its grotesque figures and for the magnificent view from the fountain terrace. Again, quite distinct and original in its formation is the Villa Gamberaia [figure 24], looking over the roofs of Florence. The spine of the narrow garden is a grass alley running the whole of its length.

Some of these Italian gardens are still alive or well restored; others less fortunate in their fate live on as ruins. Many, for instance, are the descriptions given by travellers of the Villa Borghese, which had its early seventeenth-century origins in a vineyard outside Rome owned by the Borghese family. Evelyn in 1644 called the place as an 'Elysium of delight... at a distance like a little town'. It then had a vivarium with 'estriges, peacoks, swans, cranes and divers strange beasts', and was full of 'all sorts of delicious fruits and exotic simples'. In 1789 a Scottish artist, Jacob Moore, began extensive alterations to convert this Italian scene into an English 'landskip'.

Menageries had been from early times a feature of gardens. The grotto is of later date. Its origins and psychology must be of considerable interest but here we can only refer to the elaborate construction used for them in Renaissance times. Their design was a matter for specialisation, and their changing fashions from period to period will subsequently be remarked upon. A typical example is that at the Villa Maser near Venice. It displays a massive entrance with typical symbols and figures, such as the fountain and mystic pool [figure 23].

We may conclude this fragmentary account of the Italian garden with two accounts that generalise its essential qualities. First, there is Henri Taine writing of the Villa Albani, at Rome, built by a Cardinal largely to house his antiques. 'The superb ilex rises above a terrace, with its monstrous pilasters and evergreen dome of monumental foliage. Avenues of sycamores diverge in rows shaped like porticoes. Lofty solemn cypresses clasp their knotty branches against their grey trunks and rise in the air gravely and monotonously like pyramids. The aloe stretches itself against a white wall, its strange trunk scaled and tortuous like a serpent writhing in convulsions. Beyond, outside the garden, on a neighbouring hill-side, a confused mass of structures and pines elevate themselves, rising and falling according to the surface of the ground. On the horizon runs the sharp broken line of the mountains, one of which, blue like a heavy rain-cloud, rises triangularly and shuts off a portion of the sky. From this the eye reverts back to the series of arcades forming the circular portico, to the balustrades and statues diversifying the crest of the roof, to columns scattered here and there, and to the squares and circles of the hedges and fish-pools.'

Then there is William Beckford's nocturne on an October evening of 1780 in the Boboli gardens. 'Having marked the sun's going down and all the soothing effects cast by his declining rays on every object, I went through a plot of vines to a favourite haunt of mine—a little garden of the

19 Cardinal Giovanni Francesco Gambara, Bishop of Viterbo, who created the larger part of the garden at the Villa Lante

20, 21 Two views of the garden at the Farnese Palace, Caprarola, thirty-five miles north-west of Rome. The palace and garden were made by Cardinal Alessandro Farnese in the 1550's. At the top of the picture opposite is the much admired casino, from the foot of which flows a water-shoot, or *catena d'acqua*, flanked by the two gigantic river-gods seen in closer detail in the illustration above

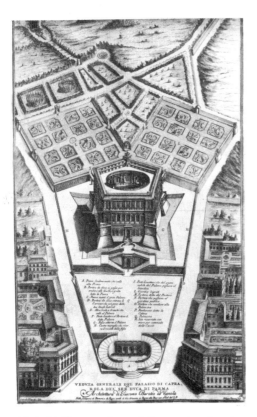

22 A bird's-eye view of Caprarola, showing the layout of a sixteenth-century Italian garden. The casino illustrated on the previous page is in the top-left corner

most fragrant roses, with a spring under a rustic arch of grotto-work fringed with ivy. Thousands of fish inhabit here, of that beautiful glittering species which come from China. This golden nation were leaping after insects as I stood gazing upon the deep clear water, listening to the drops that trickle from the cove. Opposite to which, at the end of a green alley, you discover an oval basin, and in the midst of it an antique statue full of that graceful languor so peculiarly Grecian. While I stood there, musing on the margin of the spring (for I returned to it after casting a look upon the sculpture), the moon rose above the tufted foliage of the terraces, which I descended by several flights of steps, with marble balustrades crowned by vases of aloes.'

When Italian architecture with its underlying classic calm became, as it were, lashed by the vigour of man's mind and emotion into the endlessly curling waves of baroque, we can best see its effects on garden design by moving over the Alps into Austria. From the mid-seventeenth century, Vienna, particularly in the reign of Leopold I (who reigned till 1705), become a centre of the arts. Johann Bernard Fischer von Erlach dominated the architectural scene. He had studied in Italy from 1680 to 1685, the great Bernini having died in the former year. His mastery of the three dimensions was superb, and the gardens of his great buildings were conceived in unity with them. They were contrived so that from the house the eye passed over the intimate foreground to the contrasted distance. The palace of Schönbrunn, with its tragic associations, is one of his most powerful works. The original plan was on an even vaster scale than the building that now exists. It was to stand on the site of a hunting box destroyed by the Turks — a summer palace for Leopold's son Joseph. The first plan of about 1692 placed it on a hill with the gardens falling to the River Wien below in a series of five terraces retained by arches reminiscent of those carrying the Roman aqueducts. It was to be the most magnificent baroque palace in Europe, and the effect of the terraces would have been stupendous. The original idea was abandoned, and the building, on a smaller scale (but even so immense), was erected on the river level. The main lines of the garden were very formal with a huge central courtyard contrasted with hornbeam hedges fifty feet high (clipped twice yearly).

The gardens and hot-houses round the palace were reserved for the Imperial family and contained one of the most remarkable botanical collections in Europe. With it was associated one of the most famous of all Austrian botanists, Nicolaus Jacquin (1727-1817). The 'statues of heathen gods and goddesses' are indeed a feature of these baroque gardens. At Schwarzenberg, built for Heinrich von Mansfeld, Prince of Fondi, and finished in about 1715, the statues by Lorenzo Mattei are most delicately carved and duly celebrated. The garden around them is shaded by fine trees, and from it an ascent is made to the terrace with its fine view of Vienna—a reversal of the usual principle of terrace design.

The problem now arises of placing Spanish gardens tidily within any of our categories. Few countries have been more impressed by different cultural influences. Particularly strong were those of the Visigoths and, from the long southern coast-line all but touching the African continent, the Muslim or Moorish. The latter was particularly strong, reaching far into northern Spain and carrying with it not only a style of garden design that is of a non-European kind, but a love of green as the predominant colour, and of the purple iris as a garden flower and as a theme for stylised decoration. Coming from hot climates, fountains, canals and shady arbours were a traditional necessity rather than an ornament. The sombre and perpetual green of the cypress is contrasted with the fugitive pink flowers of the Judas tree (in Spain, bearing the more apposite and pleasing name of *arbol del amor*) symbolising the lighter joys of life. The

23 The Villa Barbaro, Maser, near Venice, designed by Palladio. The view through an open window is towards the garden-house or *Ninfeo*, with its curved façade and statues

24 (*left*) The Villa Gamberaia

25 (*right*) Garden of Villa San Domenico

26 The patio of the Lindaraja, Alhambra, Spain, where the American writer, Washington Irving, lodged in the nineteenth century

27 The Casa de Pilatos, Seville. The garden is enclosed between the wings of a fifteenth-century house

oriental plane, whose beauty so affected Xerxes, is again a feature of the Spanish garden. There is another marked cultural difference between the Iberian peninsula and so much of the rest of southern Europe. It was graphically put long ago by Sir John Stirling Maxwell, who held that landscape painting was but little cultivated in Spain: 'The Vega of Granada, beautiful beyond the praise of Arabian song; the delicious 'garden' of Valencia, where the azure-tiled domes of countless convents glittered amidst their groves of mulberry, citron and palm; the stern plains and sierras of Castile; the broad valley of the Guadalquivir, studded with towered cities and goodly abbeys; the wild glens of the Alpuxarras; the pine forests of Soria, have found no Claude or Salvator to feel and express their beauty and magnificence.'

Yet in spite of these differences and singularities, Spain has strong links with Italy and so may be included here. Firstly, because Rome left her marks indelibly on the country and secondly because the final glories of Spanish architecture were inspired by baroque. The most typical feature of the Spanish garden remains of Roman origin—the patio, or internal courtyard. This is seen in the Casa de Pilatos, Seville [figures 27 and 29]. Legend says it was built as a copy of Pilate's house in Jerusalem. It is in the Mudéjar style—that is, under Moorish inspiration. Here, as is usual in Moorish design, is a garden whose compartments are divided by tiled paths which are moistened in the hot weather. There are loggias and plantings to give shade. The place must have been much the same in the days of the Duke of Alcalá who, in the sixteenth century, was a great patron of the arts and learning and was often visited by Cervantes.

The royal palace of Aranjuez is another vast place where foreign influences have become naturalised. In the first half of the sixteenth century it was only a hunting lodge built by Charles V near the River Tagus. The garden was

28 (*left*) Fronteira, Portugal, with its vast par terre, 250 foot square, of clipped box, and its 'tank' lined with blue and white *azulejo*

29 (*below*) The cool garden of the Casa de Pilatos, seen through a superb arch, rounded as if Romanesque, but decorated with Moorish designs in stone and tiles

begun by his successor, Philip II, who was responsible for introducing the English elm to form, quoting John Evelyn, 'those incomparable walks and vistas both at Aranjuez, Casal del Campo, Madrid, the Escurial and other places of delight belonging to the King and Grandees of Spain'. He wrote: 'The palace is situated on the bank of the famous River Tagus and the plantation on the north, where there is a piece of ground enclosed, formed into walks of six hundred and eighty yards long, and three hundred in breadth, in shape of a trapezium or parallelogram, about which the Tago is artificially drawn to fence it. Next to the river-side are more walks not above twenty-foot in breadth (for closer shade) planted on each side with double ranks of elm, some of which are forty yards high, stript up to the top, and so near set as fifteen-foot space: through which glides a narrow channel of water to refresh the trees.

Over the mountains from Spain to the west lies Portugal, that narrow strip anciently known as Lusitania with its long sea coast carrying the brunt of Atlantic storms and Atlantic weather. Thus, though many of the historical influences are very similar to those of Spain, the geographical and climatic differences are considerable and this inevitably affects gardening, since much of Portugal has a heavy rainfall spread over the year. The equable climate, no doubt, has resulted in a more gentle and modest architecture based largely on the Romanesque tradition. A particular

30 Queluz, near Lisbon. Part of the 'Dutch' canal, over a hundred yards long, which is lined by superb *azulejo* panels, a distinctively Portuguese form of decoration. At festival-time, the canal would be afloat with small galleys, manned by allegorical figures, and the whole garden would become a pleasure-ground

feature is the use of tiles, the *azulejos* [figure 30], which, even when the buildings or gardens are in some introduced style, inevitably results in a typically Portuguese effect. The rich vegetation that may be found in Portugal is well known from Byron's account:

Lo! Cintra's glorious Eden intervenes
In variegated maze of mount and glen...
The horrid crags, by toppling convent crown'd,
The cork trees hoar that clothe the shaggy steep,
The mountain-moss by scorching skies imbrown'd,
The sunken glen, whose sunless shrubs must weep,
The tender azure of the unruffled deep,
The orange tints that gild the greenest bough,
The torrents that from cliff to valley leap,
The vine on high, the willow branch below,
Mixed in one mighty scene, with varied beauty glow...
On sloping mounds, or in the vale beneath,
Are domes where whilome kings did make repair;
But now the wild flowers round them only breathe;
Yet ruin'd splendour still is lingering there.
And yonder towers the Prince's palace fair...

In this landscape around Cintra such exotic plants as bougainvillea, geraniums, plumbagos and acacias thrive; when in the late 1780s William Beckford had a garden here to which he introduced English plants, he described how they grew in a Jack-in-the-bean-stalk manner, and it was among these mountains that he was one of the first to rhapsodise on the beauties of an alpine flora.

Queluz, on the road from Lisbon to Cintra, has its pink rococo palace with gardens laid out by the Frenchman Jean Baptiste Robillon in the 1760s [figures 30 and 33]. An early nineteenth-century visitor described reaching it after a journey along a road lined with wild geraniums and myrtles, as a 'neat, agreeable place decorated with a variety of handsome bridges, temples, waterfalls, fishponds'. This indicates that the claim that the gardens of Queluz form the Por-

31 Lord Byron (1788-1824) in Greek costume

33

32 A grotesque dolphin
flanking a stone
fountain at Queluz

tuguese Versailles is a little off the mark; indeed, a recent
writer has called it the anti-Versailles, so picturesque is it.
Portugal triumphs over the French designer. Not only are
buildings walled with *azulejos*, but the canal is lined with
them [figure 30], formed into blue and white panels showing
fishes and sea monsters, while an *azulejo* bridge crosses it.
The many-compartmented garden in terraces and parterres
is planted with neat and complex patterns of close-cut evergreens resembling the Dutch rather than the French style.

One cannot leave Portugal without a reference to its
wealth of native plants, particularly bulbs, which have
been surprisingly overlooked until quite recently and are
now enriching gardens elsewhere.

34

33 The exquisite royal palace of Queluz, which lies five miles from Lisbon, was built in 1750 for Dom Pedro by Vicente de Oliveira, with the cooperation of the French sculptor and architect, Jean Baptiste Robillon. The great topiary parterre is enhanced by formal balustrades, terraces and statuary

CHAPTER TWO

France and

34 André Le Nôtre, the greatest of all gardeners

Le Nôtre

AN ENUMERATION OF THE singular contributions that France has made to our gardens might well begin, like that of Holland, with the trees, shrubs and plants that are among our prime and universal materials. From North America, in the early seventeenth century, and from China during the eighteenth and late nineteenth centuries, the learned and heroic Jesuit missionaries brought back rare plants. The names of any collection of so-called old-fashioned roses will alone show their provenance to be France; they are only some of the shrubs and herbaceous plants raised mostly in the nineteenth century by names still famous in plant history such as Vilmorin, Soulange-Bodin, Lemoine, Prevost, Noisette, Cayeux and many others. There the likeness to Holland ends, for as we are discussing gardens rather than plants, it is to André le Nôtre and his evolution and mastery of the formal garden in its perfection — a style that for many years dominated the civilised world— that we must give the highest honour.

Le Nôtre appeared at a fortuitous moment, since for most of his life he was able to serve that most extravagant patron of the arts, Louis XIV, who held his throne from 1643 to 1715, giving an exceptional period of uninterrupted support. Le Nôtre himself, who served one way and another in the Royal Gardens from 1643 to 1700, was the culmination of several generations of training in the practice of horticulture and the art of garden design to a standard that has never since been reached. We must, therefore, give some

35 A Swiss tapestry of the fifteenth century from Basel or Lucerne, with wild men and beasts against a background of flowers

36 The promenade of the Tuileries gardens, where Le Nôtre received his early training

account of the antecedents and traditions which nurtured him.

The gardens of mediaeval France were much like those of the rest of northern Europe. The French monastic orders had a great accumulated knowledge of herbs and the utilitarian use of plants; it was from Normandy that much gardening and plant-lore spread to the British Isles. And, in the middle part of the sixteenth century, among the religious refugees who spread the knowledge of several crafts, there were numerous Frenchmen. That in France the knowledge of plants was considerable in the fifteenth century is seen from the details of tapestries, the floral borders in the work of the court painter Jean Bourdichon (trained in the *atelier* of Jean Foucquet) and in Anne of Brittany's *Book of Hours*, produced in the opening years of the sixteenth century. At the very end of the fifteenth century Charles VIII brought back from the wars, which he fought for the crown of Naples, something of the Italian manner. But it was not until the return from captivity in Italy of Francis I in 1527 that there began 'that veritable orgy of building that flowered France with the palaces and houses of the French Renaissance: Fontainebleau, Saint-Germain, Blois... and a host of others'. What is significant from our point of view is that previously, in 1519, Francis had acquired the Tuileries—a then not very interesting estate by the Seine, but which was to become one of the most notable gardens in the world, and provide the training ground for a whole band of distinguished gardeners, of whom two, Claude Mollet and André le Nôtre, developed from Italian foundations gardens of controlled magnificence and splendour.

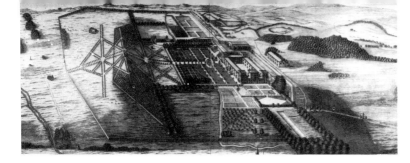

37 The formal avenues at Wilton, the seat of the Earls of Pembroke. This view of an English garden in the grand manner, drawn about 1715, well illustrates the rigidity of garden-design at this period

At first, the new gardens of royalty and nobility were no more than adaptations of the Italian manner. Balustraded terrace walks, fountains, parterres near the house, avenues radiating from it; arbours, tunelled walks, statuary, pergolas, trellis-work, mazes and grottos—all were component parts, but not yet composed into one mighty whole.

Somewhere in the pursuit of our pleasures, we must investigate one that is fundamental, if by its nature limited. Since trees lined out rigidly, as radiations from a centre, as long alley-ways, single or double, or as margins to the bosky woodlands through which one passes, are a marked feature in the sixteenth-century French gardens—though Holland was famed for them too—and onwards, this seems a suitable place to discuss avenues. What connection deep down in man's subconscious mind links these sophisticated ranks of limes and horse-chestnuts with the megalithic avenues of standing stones? And why, all of a sudden in the mid-eighteenth century should Englishmen decide with such active violence to throw down these straight rows, and other nations—fortunately to a very limited extent—follow their example? The favourite tree for this regular planting is the lime, being 'the most proper and beautiful for walks, as producing an upright body, smooth and even bark, ample leaf, sweet blossom, the delight of bees, and a goodly shade at a distance of eighteen or twenty-five foot'. France has, however, a particular interest in the horse-chestnut as an avenue tree. The *marronier d'Inde* had been introduced by a Parisian collector of rare plants named Bachelier, who brought nuts from Constantinople in 1615. The fecund nature of the species enabled Cardinal Richelieu to plant it

38 Versailles. The triumphal arch in the background is flanked by four pyramids of gilded metal and the plinths of the fountain are marble

freely in his grounds at Rueil. Le Nôtre used the horse-chestnut very extensively from about 1668, and towards the end of the century it was being planted in great numbers in the formal gardens of England. Today, used to it as we are, we surely do not adequately appreciate how this universal use has altered the aesthetics of our gardens and parks. Consider the erect, symmetrical, neat-leaved lime, or that other avenue tree, the cumbrous and stately elm; the horse-chestnut (which originates not from India or Turkey, but in a small and for long remote part of the Balkans) has, on the other hand, exotic snake-like limbs, 'like a Christmas candle-stick twisted', a broad and heavy fan of leaves, and mounting pyramids of flowers.

It is, however, to a slightly earlier period that we must return to continue the history of the Tuileries. Little was done with the new acquisition until the death of Henry II in 1559 when his widow, Catherine de Medici, proceeded — with considerable variations—to realise her late husband's plans. She had memories of Italy, and the first Tuileries designs were, as of other contemporary French gardens, very much in the Italian manner. A body of craftsmen grew up with and around the place, among whom is recorded a Le Nôtre—whether an ancestor of André seems however, uncertain. Further developments took place immediately after Henry IV succeeded in 1594, when new parterres of a much more spacious manner were made. The design of these, a break from the old Italian manner, is attributed to the Mollets, father and son: the son, Claude Mollet, tells in his famed book *Théâtre des Plans et Jardinage*, of 1652, how these were first introduced at Anet. Claude Mollet was later to become *Premier Jardinier du Roi*, to live near the Tuileries, and, under the enthusiastic Henry, to alter and add to them, in a manner showing that while Italy stood still, France was developing a new manner, broader in conception, and also producing gardeners of great skill, such as the Mollets (three generations were

40

famed: Claude's son André came to England in the time of the Commonwealth and then worked for Charles II); the Robins, father and son, two of the most skilful botanical gardeners of the day; the Le Nôtres, and such specialists as the de la Quintinies, father and son, masters of the art of fruit and vegetable culture.

Many of these men were, naturally, associated with gardens other than the Tuileries. Claude Mollet had an international reputation. But by 1608 the traveller Thomas Coryate could say that they were the most magnificent gardens that he knew, and it was in the Tuileries garden that the climax, as it were, of this French development occurred. Jean Le Nôtre was at least the second generation of gardeners of that name. When he was keeper of the great western parterres of the Tuileries, his son André was born in 1613. The boy was brought up within their precincts, and among the remarkable body of gardeners that was connected with it. Claude Mollet's wife was his godmother. He showed great ability. Serving his normal apprenticeship in gardening under its most distinguished exponents, he also studied art contemporaneously with Charles le Brun, and subsequently architecture. In due course he lived and worked in the Tuileries. Almost automatically he took his place in that galaxy that centred first round Nicolas Foucquet, and then, under Le Brun, Louis XIV. So it was he came to to design his first masterpiece, Vaux-le-Vicomte, whose untimely end has already been mentioned.

This garden may well be taken as displaying the typical manner of Le Nôtre, and as illustrating the final break with the Italian tradition, so that it is a good example to discuss [figures 3, 39, 40, 41, 44, 48 and 51]. First, however, there are some general principles. Above all is the unity of the design. The garden is considered as a whole, down to the smallest detail. There is a masterly use of levels, emphasised by the flat planes of water. The general plan is unchanging, though with countless variations within it.

39 Le Nôtre was forty-three when he began work on the huge garden at Vaux-le-Vicomte. Three villages were removed to create this vista

40 The reverse view of Vaux-le-Vicomte, across the canal, which Le Nôtre created by diverting a small river

The house stands a little raised above the garden, so that from the windows the pattern of the parterres may be relished. In front of the house is a court. Then, at right angles to, and parallel with, the long axis of the building, strikes out the huge, main vista: broad, and straight as a die. Along it first, on either side, come the parterres. Then comes an interruption, only slight, usually of water, and part of a major cross axis. The pathways bordering the vista here diverge on either side, but the obstacle overcome, continue once again on their way. The vista now leads to an architectural feature. At Vaux-le-Vicomte it is a complex matter of steps, ramps and a terrace; at tiny Melbourne in Derbyshire no more than an arbour of superbly wrought ironwork. Beyond this, a broad grassy space, tree-lined, drives the central vista still onwards into the distant landscape. On either side of this great view lie innumerable contrivances for delight, fountain gardens, bosquets, menageries, all subsidiary to, yet all united with it.

All this can be seen in the old perspective of Vaux-le-Vicomte. But it does not tell us that when Foucquet decided to build and excel all that had gone before, he chose from his properties one that seemed entirely unpropitious. It was rough, undulating woodland, carrying an insignificant manor house and three hamlets. The site chosen for the new château (which in itself, from the design of the royal architect Le Vau, is an acknowledged masterpiece) looked down upon marshy land through which flowed—across what was to be the vista—the River Almond. Beyond this, the bosky ground rose irregularly. Here Le Nôtre, taking his key from Le Vau's château, set to work. Money was unlimited; it is said eighteen thousand men were employed. Levelling, transplanting and planting of trees began on an unexampled scale. A stroke of genius was to trap all the water from the river and the little streams into the long canal which forms the major, and surprising, cross axis, and supplies the numerous minor water-works and fountains. Thus was a piece of marshy, useless land transformed. Vaux-le-Vicomte, like most of the great French seventeenth-century gardens, has no truck with Nature, however she may be defined. Le Nôtre eternally challenged and defied her—though cunningly calling in geography to aid him in her defeat. His designs might well be called abstract—even inhuman, for the exquisite ornament and sculptures are as often as not of the gods.

Le Nôtre left no plans, no record of his method. Often, Claude Mollet's *Théâtre des Plans et Jardinage* is quoted as giving the clue to the French manner. It was, however, published in 1652—nearly a decade before Le Nôtre worked at Vaux-le-Vicomte. Rather more apposite, therefore, is the work of the savant Dezallier d'Argenville, *La Théorie et la Pratique du Jardinage*, published anonymously in 1709. Particularly is this so as it went through several editions and was excellently translated into English by John James as *The Theory and Practice of Gardening*, a most influential book, yet published just at the moment when the English landscape garden was in its birth pangs.

It is fascinating, in view of the simplicity of the English manner of treating water that was so shortly to become the vogue, to repeat what d'Argenville had to say of it. 'Fountains and waterworks,' he wrote, 'are the life of a garden;

41 The skilful use of inclined planes at Vaux-le-Vicomte reveal Le Nôtre's artistry at its most ingenious

42 A pavement in pebble-mosaic in the upper terrace at Caprarola

'tis these make the principal ornament of it, and which animate and invigorate it, and, if I may so say, give it new life and spirit. 'Tis certain, that a garden, be it in other respects never so fine, if it want water, appears dull and melancholy, and is deficient in one of its greatest beauties. The distribution of water in a garden, is one of the most difficult points; it requires some ingenuity and industry to order it so that a little quantity shall appear a great deal; and that not lavishing the water away in shell-works and little basins, which are but trifles, it be spared for necessary places, where it may make a handsome effect, in forming large and well-fed spouts'. And with more precise definition, of cascades: 'they are composed of sheets, buffets, masks, bubblings, mushrooms, sheafs, spouts, surges, candlesticks, grills, tapers, and vaulted arches of water. They are accompanied with maritime ornaments, and such as are suitable to the water, as artificial ice, and rock-works, congelations, petrifyings, and shell-works, water-leaves, bulrushes and reeds imitating the natural, with which the surface of the walls and borders of the basins are lined. They are likewise adorned with figures that naturally belong to the water, as rivers, naiades or water nymphs, tritons, serpents, sea-horses, dragons, dolphins, griffins, and frogs, which are made to throw out, and vomit streams and torrents of water. This is the greatest part of what enters into their composition'. Lister wrote that the cascade at Saint-Cloud was 'said to be the most beautiful and best furnisht with water of any in France', while among the woods there was a *jet d'eau* ' which threw up a spout of water ninety-foot high... and gave now and then cracks like the going off of a pistol; such force the vent of wind in the pipes had'.

If the waterworks provided the ejaculatory part of these great gardens, the parterres contrasted it with their ornamental flatness, their even surface spreading round the house, near to which they were always laid out, so that they might be looked down upon. The parterre had been elaborated from the cruder and simpler knot—a pattern which somehow has since the earliest times fulfilled a fundamental need felt by man in his gardens. Again we can quote Lister: 'The compartments and borders of parterres are taken from geometrical figures, as well right-lin'd as circular, mix'd, etc. They take various designs into their composition, as branch'd and flourish'd work, palms, foliage, hawk's-bills, sprigs, tendrells, volutes, knots, stalks, ties, chaplets, beads, husks, cartoozes, plumes, compartiments, frets or interlacings, wreaths and shell works of grass, paths, borders, etc. And sometimes to these are added the designs of flowers, as roses, pinks, tulips and the like. Formerly they put in the heads of greyhounds, griffins, and other beasts, with their paws and talons, which had a very ill effect, and made parterres look very heavy and clouterly'. Parterres were to be above all light and un-confused in their patternings. Grass, borders of flowers, sand, brickdust, and dross from iron-smiths were some of the materials used.

Further afield, into the woods were cut pathways, terminating in 'cabinets', clearings of regular (and sometimes elaborate) geometrical shape: at their centre might stand a pond and fountain, or a lawn surrounded by trellis-work, or some other ingenuity. Wooden buildings, of complex design, but no more than uncovered wooden frames, or arbor work, were suitably sited; figures and vases were set among the horn-beam hedges that divided the parts of the garden, and 'the ends and extremities of a park are beautified with pavilions of masonry, called Belvederes or Pavilions of Aurora, which are as pleasant to rest one self in, after a long walk, as they are to the eye, for the handsome prospect they yield; they serve also to retire into when it rains'.

Iron grills extended the view at the end of long walks (yet retaining the closed-in feeling of safety) which were embellished with such plants as orange-trees, pomegranates, and myrtles standing in wooden cases. Pots of Dutch

43 Design for a garden-parterre, French eighteenth century

44 Another modern view of the garden at Vaux-le-Vicomte, now restored by the Sommier family to precisely the condition that Le Nôtre imagined

45 The Château de Beloeil, Belgium, one of the most splendid European gardens that owe their inspiration to the great French garden-designer

ware were stood on terraces, beside steps, or on stone paths on the verges of the grass. And of seats, 'you can scarce ever have too many'. In the late stages of the French garden, we read, grottos and trick perspective works were little used, especially grottos 'which are very subject to ruin'. Behind this complex organism of masonry, water, trees and plants were the hosts of skilled gardeners and workmen. Elsewhere, the fruit was grown on walls: at that time the French were past-masters at its cultivation. The pleasures of grandeur were achieved to perfection, yet at a cost that was ultimately liquidated in blood at the Revolution.

The park and gardens of the Palace of Versailles, continually changing, where Le Nôtre worked from shortly after the fall of Foucquet in 1661 (when the place was no more than a hunting box) until his death, may be regarded as the epitome, indeed a museum, of the late seventeenth-century French style: whole books have been written upon them. It may be salutary to quote the opinions of two noted Englishmen who viewed the place not long after France had been shattered and shaken by the Revolution and the defeat of Napoleon. They saw, too, through eyes by now used to gazing on the English landscape garden. In 1816 the poet Shelley summed up the magnificence abruptly: 'We saw the palace of Versailles... the gardens are full of statues, vases, fountains and colonnades ... in all that essentially belongs to a garden they are singularly deficient... the orangery is a stupid piece of expense'. So much for the romantic's view of the remains of Le Nôtre's masterpiece. Then, a little more charitable, on Christmas Eve, 1830, John Claudius Loudon found the gardens 'dreary beyond what can be imagined, when they are not filled with company; and there is not a spot or corner in them to exercise the imagination, unless it be the orangery, which contains trees of upwards of three centuries old. The water-works in these gardens are too intricate and curious to be grand, and very different

46 One of the little pavilions in the garden
of the Petit Trianon, Versailles

indeed from the two magnificent columns of water, which
rise to the height of nearly a hundred feet in front of the palace of Nymphenburg, near Munich. The pleasure of walk-
ing in these gardens is materially lessened by their sloping
surface, and in many parts of them by the want of shade.
There is a baldness in the immediate front of the palace,
which nothing can remove but an immense crowd of people; for all the arenas and courtyards at Versailles are too
large for the length of the building, at least according to
modern taste. Compared with plantations of the present
day, there is great want of variety in the sorts of trees employed; though this defect will be amply made up to those

47

47 The Latona fountain at Versailles, in which seventy-four separate jets of water poured into the central basin

who have paid but little attention to botany, by the number and diversity of the marble statues. Notwithstanding all these, and many other observations which we could make on the causes of the little pleasure afforded by these gardens when not full of company, and their inaptitude for being made the most of when filled, we should be sorry to see them neglected. Since they have been created at enormous expense, let them be kept in repair for their *mérite historique*: for the moral lesson that conveys, and for the enjoyment of the public.' Today, the wheel of taste has turned full circle. We have illustrated the comments made by these authors from old prints and modern photographs (and now add the Trianon to our selection) to indicate both the vagaries of fashion and the excelling beauty of Le Nôtre's design.

The grand manner of Le Nôtre and his master spread far beyond France. A remote example is Peter the Great's Peterhof, designed by the Frenchman Le Blond. 'Bordering on a precipice stands the palace, thereby acquiring a certain peculiar prospect over the gardens and the gulf, to the shores of Carelia and St Petersburg, and to Cronstadt... The declivity from the back front of the palace towards the sea has two magnificent cascades, rolling their streams over the terraces into large basins, and beneath which a visitor may walk as under a vault, without receiving wet, into a beautiful grotto. The whole space in front of this declivity, down to the sea-shore, is one large stately garden, famous for its *jets d'eau* and artificial waterworks. Some of them throw up columns of water, a foot and a half in diameter, to a height of two and a half or three fathoms'. So wrote a traveller of 1813, gazing open-mouthed at the wonders of the waterworks, which for number (a recent account reports a hundred and twenty-six fountains and three cascades), extent and playfulness, he considered superior to those of Versailles, [figure 124].

Le Granja in Spain has already been mentioned, while

48 One of the many sculptures by Girardon in the Garden at Vaux-le-Vicomte

49 The Pavillon française in the garden of the Petit Trianon, Versailles

automatically, as we have also seen, the fashion was taken up by numerous European princelings. In England, Charles II asked Louis for the loan of Le Nôtre to lay out his own grounds, but there is no evidence that he came. But royal gardeners included a Frenchman, André Mollet, trained in the grand manner, and an Englishman, John Rose, who had studied under Le Nôtre. George London, and his successor Henry Wise, who dominated British garden design until 1727, worked entirely in the French manner if sometimes tinged with the Dutch spirit.

All over the Continent whole gardens—true, they have often been added to or altered—remain to reflect the last rays of le Roi Soleil, except in Britain, where the land-

50 The Temple of Love in the Trianon garden

scapers swept all away in their strangely puritanical and claustrophobic manner. Here and there we may still catch a glimpse of the estates so proudly displayed in the eighteenth-century engravings, but it is usually no more than a fragment of an avenue, now marching aimlessly across the country-side towards a *pâte d'oie* that disappeared long ago. Somehow the garden at Melbourne, almost alone, has largely escaped being curved and twisted out of existence. At Studley Royal in Yorkshire the fine 'water-works' of between 1720-40 remain, but are now part of a landscaped scene. Here and there old terracing, a garden building or statuary takes us back to the great days. But always that once important feature, the ornate parterre, has disappeared and been replaced by smooth green lawns, beloved of the English.

51

51 Vaux-le-Vicomte

CHAPTER THREE

The

Gothic North

WE HAVE RATHER SKIPPED over the early history of French gardens for two reasons. First, the mediaeval garden can be more effectively illustrated by northern examples, and second, when we come to continue the story of post-mediaeval developments it will be of help to have had a preview both of Italy and the grand French manner. We should, perhaps, also have said something in advance of the English landscape style, as that too comes into our final stages in this section—but in every other respect it is better to deal with that chronologically at a later stage.

When we consider mediaeval gardens in the more northerly parts of Europe, two distinct forms emerge quite clearly, which might well be called the therapeutic and aesthetic. The former was inevitably the earlier and for long the most consequential kind; it was largely the prerogative of the monastic orders, who in their small gardens within the precincts of their monasteries cultivated plants for healing; many of them we now grow solely for ornament without even a hint of utilitarianism. The monasteries were the repositories of the knowledge, or perhaps one should say the traditions, of such writers as Aristotle and Theophrastus, which after fall of Greece and Rome had been kept alive by Syrian, Persian and Arabian translations. The progress of early botany was long hampered by the acceptance of these pre-conceived ideas, observation of fact taking a secondary place. The study of plants themselves and their cultivation was for long a minor consideration, and

2 (*left*) The west façade of the Petit Trianon, over-looking a formal garden

3 (*right*) The Virgin and Child by a Dutch painter of the fifteenth century, illustrating the fashion of raised garden-beds and cut flowers

in mediaeval times developed almost incidentally through their study as medicinal subjects. These studies resulted in the publication of the herbals, which eventually became more and more horticultural and botanical in their outlook. They now give us some idea of the plants cultivated in late mediaeval times. Even so, an eminent thirteenth-century writer like Albertus Magnus was deeply concerned with the souls of plants, and believed that if oaks or beeches were cut to the ground, the poplars that sprang up to replace them were their transmutations.

The account books of monasteries give us glimpses of the day to day running of their gardens, but not much more. As far as concerns mediaeval pleasure gardens and their development there seems to be very little contemporary written record.

There is, for example, the description of a garden in the *Romance of the Rose*, the fourteenth-century poem, versions of which are to be found in several languages (in English there is a translation by Chaucer). As it refers to the cultivation of almonds and cloves from India, cinnamon, and zedoary (*Curcum zedoaria*, a tropical plant used as a tonic and perfume), its origins must lie far south of the land where originated, in the late fifteenth century, that famous and more factual series of Flemish pictures that illustrates it. Even the account of the garden in the poem differs from that shown by the painter. The poet has a square garden, planted closely with every kind of fruiting tree, nut alleys and evergreens planted in rows—all tall, their tops interlaced, so that no sun could come through and injure the tender grass, hardly a necessity in our northern clime! On the other hand, many pictures still exist to show us that the essential feature of mediaeval European gardens was that of enclosure. Sometimes within walls—perhaps a courtyard in a palace or a castle; sometimes enclosed by woven wattle fencing, by palisading, by trellises, or, rather later, by ornamental railings. The flower-beds were small, and in the fifteenth century seem always to have been raised; sometimes, a tree was placed in the middle, and around it was planted a flowery mead. A delightfully precise view of a garden within a courtyard as the background to a Virgin and Child is seen in a fifteenth-century Netherlandish painting at Luton Hoo [figure 53]. Here we see a series of raised beds. The picture is interesting, too, as it shows an early instance of flower-painting, in which the Dutch were soon to excel. The Madonna lily inevitably appears, that mysterious flower so intimately connected with humanity since three thousand years before the birth of Christ. It is valuable to compare this with the Virgin and Child of the School of Dürer—presumably a little later, for both show the growth of the aesthetic appreciation of flowers [figure 56].

There were other uses for gardens. In them was often placed the bath—a practice that continued even in the cool climate of England down to the seventeenth century [figure 54]. Wells, conduits and fountains became frequent.

It is to the Netherlands that we should next devote our attention. In the very early days of the sixteenth century Dutch artists had removed their flower still-lifes from being mere accessories to their religious paintings and set them up in their own right—an indication of the great development in their practical gardening and floriculture. It might well be said that if Italy has provided the design of gardens, the Dutch have supplied the flowers. This was an amazing achievement which later caused William Beckford to reflect upon their unyielding perseverance in raising 'gardens from heaps of sand, and cities out of the bosom of the ocean'. The Netherlands, from the paintings, have been for so long associated with the middling-size house, that it is well to recall that there were grand gardens—such as that shown by the painter David Vinckebooms (1578-1629) at about the time when the sixteenth passed into the seventeenth century [figure 55]. This also displays those other pleas-

54 A seventeenth-century garden-bath at Packwood House, Warwickshire

55 A garden-scene by the Dutch painter, David Vinckebooms, at the beginning of the seventeenth century. From a private collection

58 Powys Castle, Montgomeryshire, owes its remarkable yew hedges and terraced garden to the Dutch influence of the Zuylestein family, to whom the property was granted by William of Orange

ures of a garden to which we have just referred, and illustrates the high, straight hedges which have always been associated with the Dutch manner. Perhaps more typical of the seventeenth-century scene is de Hooch's painting of about 1665 [figure 57]. Here in a more modest setting, are seen the beds of flowers. By then the tulip had been introduced into the country (about 1561) and the tulipomania had waxed and waned in the 1630's. The most famous flower was *Semper Augustus*. One bulb of this was sold for four thousand, six hundred florins plus a new *caros* coach complete with two dapple-grey horses. The cash was to be paid forthwith, the carriage and horses supplied within four weeks; the solitary bulb to be delivered when ready.

The Dutch traders brought plants from many parts of the world (notably the Cape, where a botanic garden was established in 1652) and that wide, warm region known vaguely as 'the Indies'. The first catalogue of the Leyden botanic garden published in 1601 listed over a thousand kinds. Clusius (later its director) was one of the earliest plant collectors, having in 1576 published an account of a tour of Spain and Portugal, whence he brought two hundred new plants. As for the larger gardens, it seems that like the ladies and gentlemen in 1634, they were 'all Frenchified in the French fashion'. The design was simple and formal, with trees planted regularly in ranks, high hedges (formed from a variety of shrubs), with pot plants, vases and statuary (often of lead) placed about. Fountains became popular. All was rather simpler than the usual French manner, and warm red brick usually replaced stone. The persistent Dutch passion for high hedges and alleyways is shown in the painting by Isaac de Moucheron (1667-1744) of a garden at Utrecht [figure 60].

The arrival of William and Mary in England in 1689 had brought the Dutch style of gardening into vogue. William Bentinck, later Lord Portland, an intimate of the new king, became Superintendent of the Royal Gardens. He brought many plants over from his own estate at Soesdyke. His deputy was George London, who had already been to France to study the gardens there. It is significant that after the peace of Ryswick in 1697, it was to France again that Bentinck took him, not Holland. (London did, however, make what appears to have been a botanical trip to Holland.) It is, nevertheless, probably due to Dutch influence that several ancient yew-hedged gardens in England exist.

The formal garden persisted in Holland for a long time in its oldest form, for the young Humphrey Repton, later to be the innovator of the picturesque landscape garden, was partly educated in that country, and in the 1760s he wrote to his parents of the gardens that he saw displayed to the gaze from canals. They had few plants, but were of old-fashioned 'embroidery' edged with box, the beds filled with red brick dust, charcoal, yellow sand, chalk, coloured ores, and spar.

Gardening in Germany—or rather the states that formed that country—was a late development. Most of the notable gardens were products of the eighteenth century, and there seems little to record earlier than the seventeenth century. There is a description of the gardens of the Castle of Heidelberg in 1620 written by Saloman de Caus—a versatile man who was drawing-master to Prince Henry, brother of Charles I of England, and who as an architect was concerned with Richmond and possibly Wilton House. He gives particular attention to the grotto (his son or nephew Isaac became an eminent constructor of them, as well as an authority on hydraulics.) It was seventy feet long and thirty-two feet broad, the inside being divided into compartments [figure 59]. One was of shell-work, the other rustic. The varieties of inventions in water needed an hour to see them all in play. Particularly celebrated was the doorway to this subterranean pleasure-ground. It was composed of twelve carved figures of animals in a setting of rusticated stonework. The origins of this clearly lay in Italy.

59 A grotto at Heidelberg Castle

60 A painting by Isaac de Moucheron (1667-1744) of a garden at Utrecht,
illustrating the Dutch preference for high hedges and the rather simpler
modifications of French garden-design

In the great period of German garden-making, the later eighteenth and early nineteenth centuries, the Italian influence had become remote, overlaid by the French manner of Le Nôtre, in turn modified by the early French version of irregularity, or *jardin anglais-chinois*, and to some extent by the truer English landscape manner. The German situation was put thus by the architect Hirschfield in 1777: 'A singular and deplorable Gallomania pervaded Germany from the prince to the peasant, which neither irony, patriotism, nor productions which show the force of our national genius could destroy: *"ainsi font les François; voila ce que j'ai vu en France"*. But now the Aurora of judgement and good taste begins to arise in our country, and the recital of the happy changes made in England ... has prepared the way for the same revolution in Germany.'

The English style did, indeed, become general; it was adopted with great fervour, and it cannot be said that German gardens have any great originality of manner; the guide books monotonously describe most of them as 'rococo'. Some thirty years after Hirschfield, Madame de Staël wrote: 'Gardens are almost as beautiful in some parts of Germany as in England... in spite of the want of wealth, and the pride of feudal dignity, there is everywhere to be remarked a certain love of the beautiful... Often, in the midst of the superb gardens of the German princes, are placed Aeolian harps, close by grottos, encircled with flowers, that the wind may waft the sound and the perfume together. The imagination of the northern people thus endeavours to create for itself a sort of Italy; and during the brilliant days of a short-lived summer, it sometimes attains the deception it seeks.'

Giving precedence in description to size, the Schloss Nymphenburg is said to be the largest baroque castle in Germany [figures 61 and 62]. It was begun, on the site of a mediaeval castle, in 1663 by the Elector Ferdinand Maria, as a present to his consort on the birth of a son, Max Emmanuel, the

61 The Nymphenburg, Munich, from a miniature by M. von Geer, 1730

65

62 The Nymphenburg, painted by Canaletto before the formal baroque garden was transformed into an English park

63 Sans Souci, Potsdam, the retreat which Frederick the Great designed for himself on the crown of a gentle hill

future conqueror of the Turks. The architect was an Italian, Agostino Barelli. Many later additions were made and it has been called the culmination of German rococo. The site is flat, surrounded by higher tableland—a matter for criticism by some authorities. The modern plan shows its accretions; even at the time von Geer painted his almost aerial view in 1730 [figure 61], the Pagodenburg of 1716 (reputedly designed by Max Emmanuel) had been added to the original design. The house and its adjoining garden are shown in greater detail in Canaletto's painting [figure 62]. Beyond the Amalienburg—a small hunting lodge—is the English garden. This was one of the additions made by Louis Sckell for the Emperor Maximilian Joseph in the late eighteenth century. Early nineteenth-century travellers were impressed by the technicalities of the two fountains with the most powerful jets in Germany. Invented by Baader, chief engineer of the Bavarian mines, they were amongst the first to be power driven. One was worked by a water-wheel and the other by steam.

Sans Souci, near Potsdam, is a very different type of garden [figures 63, 65 and 74]. It was designed for Frederick the Great as a quiet country retreat to be set in a vineyard. The architect Knobelsdorff gained this effect by placing the building on the highest of a series of terraces. The hard-working, country-loving and flute-playing Emperor insisted that he should be able to walk direct from his palace on to the terrace without descending the usual steps. The result is a famous architectural fault, for from below, the building appears to sink into the ground.

Schwetzingen is one of those gardens that inspires in people differing reactions [figure 83]. The palace is a Renaissance one, and the remaining heart of the gardens in the manner of Le Nôtre. Around this was imposed a garden in the English manner. The anonymous author of *An Autumn Near the Rhine in 1818* described the result as among the most splendid in Germany. Others, while agreeing that the ornamental buildings (which include an Indian Mosque) were substantial and picturesque, were not entirely happy. However, the artificial ruins of a Roman aqueduct were agreed to be pleasing, and the temple of Mercury well managed. All were impressed with the freedom with which the gardens were then open to the public. One walked in to its centre, when a guide quickly made his appearance and showed and explained every part in detail. There were huge orange trees in the orangery, a collection of a hundred and forty species of greenhouse heaths, great quantities of China roses, and numerous specimen trees, each correctly labelled.

Benrath, near Düsseldorf, is close beside the Rhine [figure 64]. The rococo palace was quickly built during the Seven Years War (1756-63) and the garden is notable for its wide alleyways sweeping through trees. In the English garden a rich variety of more recently introduced kinds are now used with great effect. It is much more umbrageous than other German gardens. A little higher up the Rhine valley, at Brühl, the Augustburg Schloss is rather earlier. It was built as a pleasure-palace by the Archbishop and Elector Clemens August in 1725. The gardens justify Hirschfield's charge of Gallomania, for they might well have been copied from anything by Le Nôtre.

All these German gardens that we have described are in the grand manner. Let us therefore turn to something more intimate, and quote from G. H. Lewes an account of Goethe's garden at Weimar:

'The visitor may still read the description, at once homage and souvenir, by which Goethe connected the happy hours of love with the happy hours of active solitude passed in his garden-house in the Park. Fitly the place is dedicated to the Frau von Stein. The whole spot speaks of her. Here are the flower beds from which almost every morning flowers, with the dew still on them, accompanied letters not less fresh and beautiful, to greet the beloved. Here are the beds from which came the asparagus he was so proud to

64 Benrath, near Düsseldorf; a view across the English garden towards a wing of the house

65 A grotto in the garden of Sans Souci

send to her... It was here, in this little garden, he studied the development of plants, and made many of those experiments and observations which have given him a high rank among the discoverers of Science. It was here the poet escaped from court. It was here the lover was happy in his love. How modest this garden-house really is; how far removed from anything like one's preconceptions of it! It is true that the position is one which many a rich townsman would be glad of as the site for a handsome villa: a pretty orchard and garden on a gentle slope; in front, a good carriage road, running beside a fine meadow, encircled by the stately trees of the park. But the house, a half-pay captain with us would consider a miserable cottage.'

Nothing could be further from this genteel scene than the more or less contemporaneous behaviour in the garden of the Polish palace of Lazienki. J.C. Loudon visited it in the aftermath of the Napoleonic wars. He found that the gaiety in the time of Stanislaus (who ceased to rule in 1793) was still remembered with pleasure. The building, in the Roman style, is placed on an island. 'The entry,' he wrote, 'is in one of the two wings stretching to either shore .... You arrive without seeing the lake, and on entering the orangery, its first effect is surprising and delightful. On the north shore of this lake is an open amphitheatre of stone with its orchestra on the brink of the water; and near the margin is an island of trees, which served as a proscenium. This theatre was at all times open to the public; and in addition to the ordinary exhibitions, ships and naval engagments were occasionally exhibited... The singular effects of the illuminations, the ships, and the resounding music in the woods... are still spoken of with feelings of regret.'

He goes on to describe the grounds, laid out simply with broad alleys and smaller covered paths leading to open circles of turf for dancing and music, and for tents and booths on extraordinary occasions. In several places coffee-rooms and ice cellars were established... There were two pavilions

66 The royal palace of Drottningholm, Sweden. The garden was designed by Nicodemus Tessin the Elder, who was also the architect of the house. His orderly and symmetrical layout was clearly inspired by Le Nôtre

for the king's mistresses, and another, which served as a seraglio for strangers or visitors of the king: the three being connected with the palace by arbour-like paths, or arcades of trellis work, covered by creepers... One thing deserves to be remarked, which is not to be found in any other garden in Europe. Pedestals, as if for placing statues, were ranged in different parts of the grounds... on which, on extraordinary occasions, selected living figures, male and female, were placed and taught to maintain certain attitudes.'

Finally, we move to our most northerly point and find again that France is triumphant. In Sweden the island castle of Drottningholm was begun in 1661. It is in the manner of Versailles, with a large formal water basin and a Hercules fountain. The pattern of the parterres is still beautifully seen from the windows, [figure 66]. The garden is associated with two ladies. First, Queen Hedwig Eleonora, who ruled Sweden during the childhood of her son, Charles XI, and who delighted in the castle; and later in the eighteenth century Drottningholm became the favourite resort of Frederick the Great's sister, Louisa Ulrica. She was an enthusiastic collector of antiques and objects from China and Japan, and it was she who set up the many little buildings and nooks in the garden, one entirely devoted to chinoiserie.

69

CHAPTER FOUR

Oriental

67 A dwarf tree from the Imperial collection in the Gosho Palace at Kyoto, Japan

Interlude

E. H. WILSON, ONE OF THE first plant collectors to visit the little-known districts of Western China in the opening years of the present century and to bring to the western world such a wealth of flowering plants that gardening was revolutionised, wrote a book called *China, Mother of Gardens*. It is in many ways an apt description. For whereas other early civilisations, which have developed gardening and considered the aesthetic as opposed to the utilitarian qualities of flowers, have failed to maintain their standards, China has from ancient times to the present day been a country of gardens and gardeners. To trace to its origins the history of Chinese gardens is outside our scope. Nor was its influence on the art of European garden design at any time considerable until the late eighteenth century. On the other hand, as we have already mentioned, plants now known to have originated in China found their way to the west along the caravan routes at an early stage. These plants were by no means wild plants, but selected forms or hybrids chosen and anciently cultivated by gardeners. The black mulberry and the peach are examples.

Japanese gardening has likewise been important and continuous over a long period. It began rather later, developing under the Chinese culture introduced during the Sui and Tang dynasties, during the seventh century, and to this day is maintained at a very high level of artistry and horticultural skill.

The early Chinese interest in the aesthetic quality of plants

68 The Rikugien garden, Tokyo. It is a typical garden of the Japanese feudal period, originally laid out by Yanagisawa Yoshiyashu in the early years of the eighteenth century, and now a public park

and gardens as distinct from their utilitarian and medicinal value is shown in many references. A delightful poem written by Po-Chu-i (772-846), *Planting Flowers on the Eastern Embankment*, has become quite well known. In it he describes his plantation of a hundred flowering bushes, all mixed up together, making a thousand branches that he observes flowering in their due rotation as he sits languidly under their shelter, below him a stream and a terrace (which he enjoys sweeping), watching also the bees and the birds. Just about the time when the Normans were conquering England, Chou-Tun-i wrote of a certain T'ao Yüang-ming who in the past alone devoted himself to the chrysanthemum. From the opening days of the T'ang dynasty, he adds, the peony has been the favourite of all mankind. For his part, the stainless water-lily rising from its slimy bed, an emblem of purity reposing on the clear pool, spotless, symmetrical, with a subtle perfume wafted far and wide, is superior; the chrysanthemum, he considers, is the flower of retirement and culture; the peony the flower of rank and wealth; and the water-lily the Lady Virtue beyond compare.

Chinese skill in floriculture is shown in the observations of a certain Ch'en Hao-tsz', an amateur who wrote in 1688 of such matters as acclimatising plants brought from far countries, stratification of seeds, air-layering and manuring, all in a manner far in advance of European practice at the time, though one must add that this was mixed with a good deal of superstition comparable with our own at that period.

In mediaeval Europe little enough was known of China, though some slight link was always maintained. Marco Polo's account of his travels made in the second half of the thirteenth century was generally discredited. He wrote little about gardens, but he describes as something novel the avenues of trees closely planted along the roadsides. (He also refers to the giant hunting dogs of Tibet, which were murderously set to pursue George Forrest during his plant collecting journey of 1905). Such contact that existed was through the French Jesuit missionaries. In the late-nineteenth and early-twentieth centuries they were largely responsible for the botanical discoveries in western China that so greatly affected gardening. But long before that they were active, and Père Attiret's description of the Emperor of China's palace and garden at Pekin made in 1757 is one of the earliest accounts sent to Europe. Of the garden he wrote: 'There are Houses about the Banks of the Water, very well disposed; with their different Courts, open and close Porticos, Parterres, Gardens and Cascades; which when viewed all together, have an admirable effect upon the eye. They go from one of the Valleys to another, not by formal strait Walks as in Europe; but by various Turnings and Windings, adorned on the sides with little Pavilions and Charming Grottos; and each of these Valleys is diversified from all the rest, both by their manner of laying out the Ground, and in the Structure and Disposition of its Buildings.

'All the Risings and Hills are sprinkled with Trees; and particularly with Flowering Trees, which are here very common. The sides of the Canals, or lesser Streams, are not faced (as they are with us) with smooth Stone, and in a straight Line; but look rude and rustic, with different Pieces of Rock, some of which jut out, and others recede inwards; and are pleased with so much Art, that you would take it to be work of Nature. In some Parts the Water is wide, in others narrow; here it serpentises, and there spreads away, as if it was really pushed off by the Hills and Rocks. The Banks are sprinkled with Flowers, which rise up even through the Hollows in the Rock work, as if they had been produced there naturally. They have a great variety of them, for every season of the year.

'Beyond these streams there are always Walks, or rather Paths, paved with small Stones; which lead from one Valley

69 The garden of Katsura Rikyu, the Imperial villa of the Japanese Mikados. It is attributed to Kobori Enstru (1579-1647) and is regarded as the highest achievement of his art

70 'China — Mother of Gardens'. A French mid-nineteenth-century view of a garden in China

to another. These Paths too are irregular; and sometimes wind along the Banks of the Water, and at others run out wide from them'.

In the same year, the English architect William Chambers, who had quitted the service of the Swedish East India Company in 1749 to become an architect, brought out a book of Chinese designs for buildings, based on accurate drawings he had made while there. Apart from the pagoda in Kew Gardens, however, he worked in the classical manner. He also produced in 1772 a *A Dissertation on Oriental Gardening* which was not quite so factual and which was also a disguised attack on 'Capability' Brown. The result of this news from China was *chinoiserie* rather than a true understanding of Chinese gardening, which was a system followed not only in the Emperor's palace but in the smaller home. It was to produce (so modern scholars tell us) in close context with the house, a natural microcosm — not an imitation of nature, but a distillation of the underlying fundamental elements of nature such as stone, flowing water, still water, ancient and flowering trees all viewed from many aspects by meandering paths. The plants used for this were not generally grown in the West until well on in the nineteenth century: conifers, bamboos, bananas, flowering plums and cherries, chrysanthemums and peonies were among them. Most had symbolic meaning.

Irregularity as such, without any understanding of its nature, probably became known (under the odd name of *sharawadgii*) not from China but Japan, somewhere in the late seventeenth century through the Dutch trading connections with that country. The naturalist Kaempfer was in Nagasaki from 1690-92 attached to the Dutch East India Company and gave an early account of a Japanese garden:

'The Garden is the only place we Dutchmen, being treated in all respects little better than prisoners, have liberty to walk into. It takes in all the room behind the house, it is commonly square, with a back door, and walled in very

74

neatly like a cistern or pond, for which reason it is called *Tsubo*, which in the Japanese language signifies a large water-trough or cistern. If there be not room enough for a garden, they have at least an old ingrotted plane, cherry or apricock tree. The older, the more crooked and monstrous this tree is, the greater value they put upon it. Sometimes they let the branches grow into the rooms...

'If the *Tsubo* or Garden be a good one, it must have at least thirty-foot square and consist of the following essential parts. One: the ground is partly cover'd with roundish stones, of different colours, gather'd in rivers or upon the sea-shore, well-wash'd and clean'd, and those of the same kind laid together in form of beds, partly with gravel, which is swept every day, and kept clean and neat to admiration, the large stones being laid in the middle, as a path to walk upon, without injuring the gravel, the whole in a seeming but ingenious confusion. Two: some few flower-bearing plants planted confusedly, tho' not without some certain rules. Amidst the plants stands sometimes a *Saguer*, as they call it, or scarce outlandish tree, sometimes a dwarf-tree or two. Three: a small rock or hill in a corner of the garden, made in imitation of nature, curiosly adorn'd with birds and insects, cast in brass, and placed between the stones, sometimes the model of a temple stands upon it, built, as for the sake of the prospect they generally are, on a remarkable eminence, or the borders of a precipice. Often a small rivulet rushes down the stones with an agreeable noise, the whole in due proportions and as near as possible resembling nature. Four: a small bush, or wood, on the side of the hill, for which the gardiners chuse such trees, as will grow close to one another, and plant and cut them according to their largeness, nature, and the colour of their flowers and leaves, so as to make the whole very accurately imitate a natural wood, or forest. Five: a cistern or pond, as mention'd above, with alive fish kept in it, and surrounded with proper plants, that is such as love a wat'ry soil,

71 A raked sand-garden, for meditation, at the Tofukuji Monastry, Japan

75

72 The *Shokintei* or 'Pine-lute pavilion' of the Imperial villa at Katsura, a beautiful example of the oriental use of stone and clear water, by Kobori Enstru. The story goes that when Kobori was commissioned to lay out the garden, he made his patron promise three things: first, to set no limit on expenditure; second, never to hurry the work; and third, not to visit the garden before its completion, lest he should be tempted to proffer suggestions which might hamper the free execution of the plan conceived by the designer

and would lose their beauty and greenness if planted in a dry ground. It is a particular profession to lay out these gardens, and to keep them so curiously and nicely as they ought to be, as I shall have an opportunity to shew more at large in the sequel of this history. Nor doth it require less skill and ingenuity to contrive and fit out the rocks and hills above mention'd according to the rules of art.'

And of the garden flowers he gleaned with difficulty some information:

'Japan I think may vie with most, if not all, known Countries, for a great variety of beautiful plants and flowers, wherewith hath most liberally adorn'd its fields, hills, woods, and forests. Some of these they transplanted into gardens, and improv'd by assiduity and culture to the utmost, and indeed to a surprizing degree of perfection....'

It is of interest to observe that many plants long believed to be native of Japanese gardens have since been discovered as natives only of China, sometimes from the most remote parts in the west and centre.

These accounts of China and Japan by writers literally 'cabin'd, cribb'd, confin'd' yet give us a picture of most wonderful gardens planted with a rich variety of flowers developed over centuries. It is therefore not inconsequent to quote a more or less contemporary account of a garden in another early centre of garden art and horticulture. In 1686 Sir John Chardin wrote of Persia: 'After what I have said of the number and beauty of the flowers in Persia, one might easily imagine that the most beautiful gardens in the world are to be found there; but this is not at all the case. On the contrary, by a rule I find very general where nature is fertile and easy, art is coarser and more unknown, as in this matter of gardens. This happens from the fact that when Nature is so excellent a gardener, if I may so express it, there is nothing for art to do. The Gardens of the Persians consist commonly of a grand alley or straight avenue in the centre, planted with plane (the zinzar, or Chenar of the

East), which divides the garden into two parts. There is a basin of water in the middle, proportionate to the garden, and two other lesser ones on the two sides. The space between them is sown with a mixture of flowers in natural confusion, and planted with fruit trees and roses; and this is the whole of the plan and execution. They know nothing of parterres and cabinets of verdure, labyrinths, terraces and such other ornaments of our gardens. The reason of which is, that the Persians do not walk in their gardens, as we do; but content themselves with having the view of them, and breathing the fresh air. For this purpose they seat themselves in some part of the garden as soon as they come into it, and remain there till they go out.'

By the Time Sir John was writing, the old garden art of Persia had already lost its vitality.

The truth is that practically nothing was known of Chinese horticulture (and plants are a very important part of their gardening) until Robert Fortune went there in 1843 to collect: the instructions given to him by men who had lived there for years, still confined in their movements, indicate the state of ignorance. Japan was even more secretive; not until 1860 were their gardens and plants observed with freedom, though Philip von Siebold, by ruses and stratagems, had previously collected many Japanese plants while in the service of the Dutch East India Company.

Thus we arrive at the position that though Chinese and Japanese influence on European gardens from the eighteenth century onwards was not inconsiderable, it was largely the influence of a myth based on a few clues picked up in a handful of ports. Fortune's disillusionment with the true Cathay when he landed in July 1843 was revealing: 'Was this, then, "the flowery land", the land of camellias, azaleas, and roses of which I had heard so much in England?', he wrote in disgust. Yet, within a year or two he brought to Europe many fine plants that we now take for granted. The Chinese influence until then was no more than a de-

73 The sand-garden at the Ryoanji Temple, Kyoto, attributed to Mark Soami, and greatly influenced by Zen philosophy

76 (*right*) Part of the Chinese gardens at Biddulph, in Staffordshire, made by James Bateman in the 1840's

74 Japanese figures by Benkert and Heymüller at Sans Souci, Potsdam

75 Büring's Japanese tea-house at Sans Souci, 1755. The two figures in the upper illustration on this page show how the design was executed. The Japanese fashion was introduced into Germany from England during the rococo period

lightful *chinoiserie*, the same that we have in rococo 'Chinese' decorations applied in rooms designed to Palladian rules. In England we see it at its best in Chambers' pagoda at Kew, or scathingly shown as the spindly bridge spanning the meandering stream in Payne Knight's mocking version of Brown's 'shaven lawns'. We find it in Germany at Sans Souci [figure 75], in Poland at Lazienki near Warsaw, and often in France. Nor should we forget it (carried out in cast-iron) at Alton Towers in England [figures 78 and 103].

In the middle of the nineteenth century some serious attempts to build Chinese gardens with understanding and using Chinese plants were made. Mostly, they have disappeared, but something of one remains. James Bateman, a wealthy and learned man of Biddulph in Staffordshire, and one of the great early authorities on orchid culture, made a remarkable garden in the 1840's in which he included an area that he called simply 'China' [figure 76].

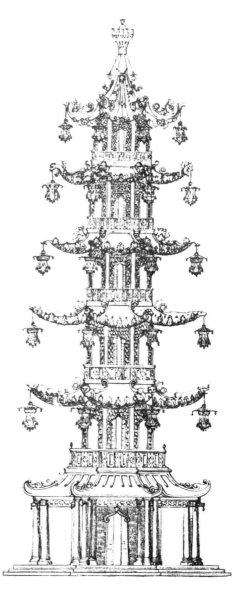

For long, *japonoiserie* was inevitably confused with *chinoiserie*. The cult of the Japanese began in the 1860's and was much more fully understood than the earlier cult of the Chinese thanks to Japanese prints and enthusiasts such as the de Goncourts. It resulted in a number of Japanese gardens in the West, often constructed by Japanese brought over for the purpose. There is little doubt that this more scholarly cult had a considerable effect on our gardens indirectly through the western artists who were influenced by it. Rarely, however, does one find anything other than remains of the late nineteenth and early twentieth century Japanese gardens that were so carefully constructed. Unfortunately the bamboos and polygonums [figure 77] that furnished them are of singularly rampant, indeed uncontrollable, growth. In a Europe torn by wars, they have long gained the upper hand. All we may see now is an occasional battered stork or stone lantern in the undergrowth.

78 The Chinese pagoda at Alton Towers, England

CHAPTER FIVE

Le Jardin

79 William Shenstone (1714-63), poet and landscape gardener. A portrait by Edward Alcock

Anglais

ANDRÉ LE NOTRE DIED in 1700, almost forty years after he had become acknowledged as the master of garden design. Balance, proportion and regularity were the components he used; nature was something rather alarming, to be kept in the distance. The pleasures of gardens were established; the rule of taste undeviating, the range of emotions equally confined.

Except, it seems, for one man, Charles Howard, Earl of Carlisle. For him Sir John Vanbrugh built the baroque Castle Howard, to be surrounded by gardens planned by George London. But in Wray Wood, sometime about 1700, 'where Mr London designed a star, which would have spoiled the wood, ... his Lordship's superlative genius prevented it, and to the great advancement of the design, has given it that labyrinth-diverting model we now see it'. So wrote Stephen Switzer, by 1718 an advocate of the new and revolutionary English 'irregularity'. Howard, no doubt, was an individual and incipient symptom among several in this epidemic of claustrophobia. At that stage, and in Switzer's plans, it is now difficult to see anything alarmingly new; for example, in his plan for Paston we are dealing with little more than irregularity alone, not the violent change that soon led to the development of the 'landskip', which in turn passed into the picturesque and the romantic. Historians of taste, and (because it altered the British landscape) an occasional historical geographer, refer to this change. Yet no one has attempted to analyse the

80 William Kent, who imported 'Italian landscape' into the English countryside

81 Woburn Farm, Weybridge. A *ferme ornée* developed by Philip Southcote

volte face in emotions that took place within a decade or two. The facts are simple: two or three professional gardeners and a number of literary persons, of whom notably Addison (who was not a gardener) and Pope (who was) substituted a whole new aesthetic, a wide new series of pleasures, to replace the thousand fountains of Versailles that now cast their 'tortured waters to the distant heavens'. Instead:

> Some sedgy flat, where the late ripened sheaves
> Stand brown with unblest mildew, 'tis the bed
> On which an ample lake in crystal peace
> Might sleep majestic...

The mile-long avenue was felled, and the poet now murmured ecstatically of his

> Smooth, simple Path! whose undulating line,...
> Plain in its neatness, spans my garden round.

Irregularity being achieved, and the pleasures of that charming but rather variably defined personage Nature having entered into the forefront of our emotions, the next stage was the return from Italy in 1719 of William Kent, a coach-painter who had made good as an artist, architect and decorator with the wealthy and dictatorial Earl of Burlington as his patron. Their joint achievement was utterly delightful and hopelessly incongruous. They set the go-ahead English peers and gentlemen to live in villas designed to the strict rules of Palladio, surrounded not by the formality of the Italian garden, but by an imitation of the temple-scattered Italian campagna as seen in the paintings of such painters as Claude, or the bosky wilderness of a Salvator Rosa. The whole dream they thus materialised was laden—for the movement was a literary one—with classical and literary allusions. (Today, with the virtual disappearance of the classical education, we are no more able to savour in full the true pleasures of the early landscape garden than we are, say, the Chinese).

While William Kent was recreating his Italian landscapes among the gentle undulations of a cool and showery

England, other landscapers were working in rather different manners. Philip Southcote at Woburn Farm near Weybridge (no connection with that Woburn in Bedfordshire where the Russell family—also great gardeners—have lived so long) was tastefully ornamenting and surrounding his property with irregular plantations of exotic trees, shrubs and flowers mingled with the native plants [figure 81]. This venture attracted the name *ferme ornée*, though it had nothing to do with France. At Painshill, also in Surrey, Charles Hamilton did the same thing on a much larger scale, forming and furnishing large artificial lakes in a serpentined, allegedly natural, manner. He, too, sprinkled his grounds with buildings and artificial grottos in a variety of architectural styles that accorded with the appropriate spiritual genius felt to inhabit each spot. Hamilton was rightly so proud of his work that he hired out carriages for the use of his many visitors. A comparable garden, more or less contemporaneous with Painshill, is Stourhead in Wiltshire [figures 82, 84 and 89]. Although its outlines and great lake, and the utterly delightful and fanciful ornamental buildings, are as Henry Hoar planned them around his Palladian mansion, their aspect has changed entirely. Generation after generation has added to the planting, using the latest introductions of trees and shrubs. So it is that most of the conifers, maples, rhododendrons and azaleas that today delight the visitor were quite unknown in the eighteenth century. This has been criticised by the ill-informed who are unaware of the tradition founded so early by Southcote, Hamilton and Hoar of planting the most recently introduced exotics; Hamilton and his gardener, Mr Thorburn, were, indeed, famed as introducers and planters of new trees and shrubs, particularly rhododendrons and azaleas of whose ultimate effect they could not have any idea. How great would be their pleasure in the luxurious foliage and infinite variations in form of the American and oriental conifers, and the complexities of coloured patterns built up with Chin-

82 A Palladian temple at Stourhead, Wiltshire, Henry Hoar's prototype garden in the new 'natural' style that so profoundly affected English garden-design

83 Schwetzingen, a German garden in the traditional French taste

84

84 Stourhead, Wiltshire. Nineteenth-century rhododendrons against an eighteenth-century garden-temple

85 A chestnut, in the manner of Salvator Rosa, craving alms of the sun with its dying branches

86 Audley End. A park-garden by Capability Brown, illustrating his manner of linking garden with countryside by the expedient of placing a temple at the end of a vista

ese rhododendrons, if they could but temporarily exchange their heavenly for their earthly paradises!

It will be seen that there are three strands in the thread of the so-called 'landskip' or natural garden. First came little more than irregularity, often imposed on an existing formal garden (as at Stowe). Then came the style of William Kent, based on literary and pictorial origins, a style of swelling curves and smooth undulations of the land, with artificial lakes contrived to simulate winding rivers (or, as at Rousham, Oxfordshire—the perfect surviving example of a Kent landscape—a real serpentining river fortuitously in existence). In it the greens and browns of the grass and trees, the billowing of rounded oaks, the boskiness of Salvatoresque, gnarled chestnuts, or the sharper accents of a pine or spruce, were preponderant. Finally, there was the much more exciting and original planting in the manner of Southcote, a style which was almost eclipsed with the arrival on the scene of Lancelot ('Capability') Brown with his early work at Warwick Castle in the late 1740s.

Brown, unlike Kent, was a most capable gardener, with a wonderful eye for forming and planting a landscape. He worked in the style of Kent, achieving a monotonously high standard, yet failing in all but a few instances to touch the real triumphs of a genius. Under his gentlemanly, dictatorial instructions avenues fell to the axe; cosy, walled gardens were flung open to the winds and parterres disappeared under acres of sheep-mown grass. Against this, England became dotted with countless charming lakes, awkward acclivities in parks were smoothed away, and thousands of acres of woodland, its margins conforming to the contours of the land, were brought into being. Brown was, too, the master of the ha-ha, that simple dry ditch, well known to the French formal school, which invisibly divided the garden proper from the surrounding countryside. Consequently he became a master of space in a new manner: a temple could be set far away (as at Audley End,

Essex) to catch the eye and lead it over a contrived, smooth scene into the countryside. Brown quickly saw the capabilities—hence his nick-name—of forming these spacious idealised landscapes, after a ride round the property on his horse. His material was the raw land. Le Nôtre produced his spaciousness by sitting down at a drawing board and working it out as an abstract idea formed by architecture; his materials were water, trees, buildings and sculpture—all fashioned by man.

So great was what we may call this epidemic of claustrophobia (many imitators followed the prescriptions of Brown) that the British scene was largely altered. His huge areas of 'shaven lawn', his winding paths and pleasant lakes were well suited to the English taste of the day, which disliked excitement and the exceptional. Today it is often difficult to disentangle Brown's work from natural park scenery: look, for example, at Ingestre in Staffordshire [figure 87], Ragley in Warwickshire and Berrington in Herefordshire where his landscapes are well preserved. His most dramatic work was at Blenheim Palace near Oxford. Here he swept away Henry Wise's great formal garden designed to suit the house (a modern formal garden now regains some of its effect) but with a stroke of genius flooded the little valley spanned by Vanbrugh's causeway, so greatly emphasising its grandeur and adding to the dignity of the scene. Brown's most lavish undertaking was at Croome, Worcestershire, for Lord Coventry. There, on a marshy site near the confluence of the Rivers Avon and Severn, he laid out grounds and planted them in a more varied manner than usual—his patron was a collector of trees—at a cost (it was said) of four hundred thousand pounds.

Before we leave this period, we must once again refer to the delightfully incongruous buildings scattered about the landscaped contours, each designed to call up the correct emotions in persons of sensibility. Such are Rousham's arcaded Praeneste and Townesende's temple now embow-

87 Ingestre, Staffordhire, another park by Capability Brown, which is now difficult to distinguish from the surrounding countryside

88 Blickling Hall, Norfolk. A garden in the grand eighteenth-century manner, with lawns leading down to a lake that disappears round the bend of a wood

89 Stourhead, Wiltshire, the first of the English 'natural' gardens. A stone bridge crosses the lake, and a temple is sited at the point where the garden melts into the countryside

90 Great Barr Hall, Staffordshire, as it appeared in about 1830, having open landscapes in the style of Humphry Repton. This is an
excellent example of the Reptonian manner

91 The Palladian bridge at Wilton, near Salisbury, completed for the Earl of Pembroke in 1737: a brilliant adaptation of an Italian style to the English scene

92 The romantic *jardin anglais* or 'Petit Hameau', made for Marie Antoinette in the grounds of the Petit Trianon at Versailles

ered with trees; Lyttleton's sham mediaeval castle at Hagley; Lord Pembroke's Palladian bridge at Wilton [figure 91], and the more monumental buildings in the rolling grounds of Castle Howard in Yorkshire. In every form and style, from belvederes to Chinese pagodas, they lie about the land. Grottos came back into favour, no longer massive, but fanciful—indeed, rococo, such as the delightful example at Weybridge in Surrey (now destroyed).

The landscape style of gardening lent itself to a good deal of absurdity. George Mason, a distinguished amateur of the classics, who was able, thanks to a successful interest in insurance, to indulge his own pleasures in landscaping, wrote in 1768: 'From a general view of our present gardens in populous districts, a stranger might imagine they were calculated for a race of Lilliputians. Are their *shade*, their *ponds*, or their *islands* proportionable to common mortals? Their winding walks—such as no human foot-step (except a reeling drunkard's) could have traced. Yet, these in the eyes of the proprietors, are perfect models of Chinese'. It was this kind of thing, rather than the true landscape. that spread to Europe, at first into France under the peculiar name of *Anglo-Chinois*. The English Garden at Le Petit Trianon, laid out for Marie Antoinette, was an early and famous instance [figure 92]. In 1787 Arthur Young visited it, and it is interesting to recall his views on the French manner of carrying out the English style. It had, he wrote, more of Sir William Chambers and chinoiserie than Brown, more effect than nature, more expense than taste—with woods, rocks, lawns, lakes, rivers, islands, cascades, grottos, walks, temples and even villages. To his mind, its glory was the exotic trees and shrubs: 'The world has been successfully rifled to decorate it; here are curious and beautiful ones to please the eye of ignorance, and to excercise the memory of science...' In 1816, after the Revolution, the poet Shelley had no more to say of them than that they were extremely pretty.

There is little doubt that when at first the French fell so heavily for the English garden, and suffered an acute *anglomanie*, they were misapprehending the true nature of the English invention. Horace Walpole outspokenly said so when he visited France in 1771. J. C. Loudon, well steeped in the true landscape tradition, also visited that country in 1828 and collected much information about the gardens, some of which had disappeared in the Revolution. He was friendly with the Scots gardener, Thomas Blaikie, who in 1776 took service with the Comte de Lauragais and was, except for the period of the Revolution (which he survived), continually making gardens in the English manner. Loudon considered that the first true example of it was at Ermenonville [figure 93], laid out by Girardin in the 1770s. This view is confirmed by the Franch *architecte paysagiste* Jean-Marie Morel, author of *Théorie du Jardin* of 1776. Loudon, indeed, considered that in its prime Ermenonville was superior to many English gardens. The château was placed on an island in the lake. Other objects of interest were Rousseau's cottage, his tomb on the Island of Poplars, and that of G. F. Meyer, an artist who helped Girardin, on another island. The picturesque effect of every object was carefully considered, not in exclusion of, but in connection with, their utility. Girardin was in pursuit of *paysages interessants*. An account of Ermenonville written in 1778 describes the garden at that time. Girardin kept a band of musicians, who constantly perambulated the grounds, making concerts sometimes in the woods, and at others in scenes calculated for particular seasons, so as to draw the attention of visitors to them at the proper moment. At night these musicians returned to the house, and performed in a room adjoining the hall full of company. Madame Girardin and her daughters were clothed in common brown stuff, *en amazones*, with black hats, while the young men wore '*habillements le plus simples et le plus propres à les faire confondre avec les enfants des campagnards*'.

93 A French adaptation of the new English style in gardens. The garden at Ermenonville by Giradin, 1770. In the centre is Rousseau's tomb on the Island of Poplars

94 This drawing, and the one opposite, both by Richard Payne Knight, illustrate the reaction against Capability Brown's 'false refinement'. Above is Knight's caricature of a Brown landscape, which he called 'suave and dull'

Loudon saw the relics of this garden in 1828, but soon after it was in ruins. It is important, as a typical example of numerous gardens in Europe that attempted to achieve the landscapes devised by the English not only in France, but particularly in many parts of Germany, Denmark (where Dronningard and Monsieur Hauch's *ferme ornée* on Esrom Lake were famed), and in Russia, where Catherine II inevitably followed the fashion, and even at Peterhof, when a Mr Meader, late gardener at Syon House, 'provided a small specimen of English gardening'. Indeed Russia, of all unlikely places, was to show an extreme example of *anglomanie*. Field Marshal Prince Potemkin employed a gardener named Gould who had worked under 'Capability' Brown. On one of the prince's journeys into the Ukraine, Gould attended him with several hundred assistants from his estate in the Crimea. When the expedition halted, if only for a day, the prince's travelling pavilion was erected and surrounded by a garden in the English taste, composed of trees and shrubs, divided by gravel walks, and ornamented with seats and statues all carried forward with the cavalcade. (Gould's successor was another Briton named Call. To make a study of the numerous English, or possibly mostly Scots, gardeners who in the late eighteenth and early nineteenth centuries were employed overseas in carrying out the English style, as well as showing their skill as cultivators of grass lawns and particularly of fruit, is a project we recommend to some student of taste).

The British Isles had at that time achieved a very high standard of horticultural skill, particularly in cultivating new and rare exotic plants. In 1787 Curtis's *Botanical Magazine*, a pioneer of scientific horticulture, first appeared: it continues to this day. But in the landscape garden flowers and fruit took no place. They were grown within walls carefully secreted so as not to impede the view.

Lancelot Brown died in 1783, still working and full of honour, his landscapes (not his writings, for they are no more than correspondence) having affected the course of gardening far beyond his native land. He was literally succeeded by Humphry Repton, who had access to Brown's papers. The succession, however, took place in an extraordinary manner. Unlike 'Capability', who worked his way up from the bottom, Repton was born into a successful middle-class family. He travelled in youth, was an amateur of all the graces, of literature, architecture, of local history in East Anglia, and was quite a talented draughtsman. He engaged, not very successfully, in business enterprises. One of these had failed at the time Brown died, and Repton was hard up. Overnight, he decided to take Brown's place; within a short while he had succeeded in so doing. His approach soon came to differ fundamentally from Brown's, though superficially the result was often similar. When working on an estate, he first made a careful and logical analysis of its inherent qualities: its situation, history, the existing house—in fact, he sought out the genius of the place. It was this he tried to use and develop, rather than enforce a rigid system upon it. Working less and less in the Brown landscape manner, he tried to produce a house set in surroundings which in themselves formed a work of art; he was not trying to produce an echo of a Claude or Poussin picture, but a new artistic entity. He was undoubtedly influenced by two friendly critics, Sir Uvedale Price and Richard Payne Knight, wealthy and highly cultured squires living in Herefordshire, on the Welsh borders. They both regretted Brown's destruction of the old formal gardens and they both objected to the suaveness of his work; they called for vigour and roughness in texture, the use of colour other than the eternal green, and the introduction of 'picturesque' scenery, with dramatic incidents to enliven the 'false refinement' [figures 94 and 95]. That these two men lived on the wild and hilly Welsh marches, so different from the quiet southern and midland counties in which Brown and his imitators usually worked, may

95 Here is Payne Knight's view of the same scene as in figure 94, redesigned according to his view of the 'ideally picturesque', with dramatic incidents inserted to enliven the view. The nineteenth century is clearly within sight

96 Another pair (with figure 97 opposite) of contrasting scenes, before and after improvement. Above is Endsleigh Cottage as Repton found it, a roughly landscaped garden overlooking the River Tamar

have had an enlivening effect; such qualities as 'grandeur' —hardly existing in Brown's belts and clumps—were now being called into play. Brown worked by eye: he rode, saw and planned. Repton worked by forming a detailed, finished picture. First, he prepared a drawing of the place as it was, and then superimposed upon this one showing how he felt it should look. More and more he brought formality back to where we now consider its right place, near the house. Flower-beds reappeared. In his last works he looked far ahead; the history of the best in garden art seems to leapfrog from him to the late nineteenth century with the coming of William Robinson and Miss Jekyll.

Many of Repton's gardens still exist: Tatton Park in Cheshire, Ruddings Park in Yorkshire, Luscombe in Devon, and Sheringham Hall in Norfolk. He wrote and drew copiously, so that we know without doubt his views and aims; we can, too, see them developing and becoming more complex. He has been a direct influence on North American landscaping, his writings having been published in the United States by Andrew Downing. His work probably reached its climax in the grounds of Endsleigh Cottage [figures 96 and 97], built as a country house in 1810 for one of the several Dukes of Bedford (or, perhaps in this case his Duchess) who, down the ages, have been great patrons of gardening, botany and natural history. The place is in the valley of the River Tamar. Repton gives the key to the setting: this stream, he tells us, suggests a tranquil river in its lower parts, where the seafarer, safe from danger, enters its placid, navigable waters from Plymouth. But at Endsleigh, a 'sol-

itude enbosomed in all the sublimity of umbrageous majesty, looks down on the infant river, struggling through its rocky channel, and hurrying onwards with all the impetuosity of ungoverned youth...' This was the site that Repton linked to the *cottage ornée*. First, it is of interest to note that Repton's paths and valleys were so designed to provide for, and display, a great variety of rare, exotic trees and shrubs; within a decade or two of his death certain choice specimens were already exciting interest. It would seem that Repton had an instinct that, in the years succeeding his death, countless new varieties as yet unknown to him would be brought into cultivation (as they were from western North America, South America, China and Japan) to be planted in, and elaborate, the scene he had set for them. Thus he foreshadowed one of the joys of the twentieth-century garden, the varied and flowering woodland. Within sight of the house, he formed a bluff into a long grass terrace, banked behind with a raised bed for rock and lesser plants: a precursor of our table garden. In the even more formal parts near the house his ingenuity was great: in one spot, a small box-edged 'old-fashioned' country garden stands on a raised, curved terrace—in whose balustrade is a runnel of water. Here is geometrical gardening of the first order, particularly as in miniature it echoes the sweep of the horizon.

Repton was looking ahead to a vision that did not materialise until, after a period of confusion, it eventually re-appeared. With him ended England's first great contribution to the art and pleasure of gardening, the artificial 'landskip', known internationally as *le jardin anglais*.

97 Endsleigh, as Repton proposed to improve it. On the right, his *cottage ornée*, which he built for the Duke of Bedford, and, centre, his long grass terrace. 'It is geometrical gardening of the first order'

CHAPTER SIX

Nineteenth-Centu

y Variety

IN THE VERY YEARS that Humphry Repton was creating his final masterpiece in landscape for Georgiana, Duchess of Bedford and her Duke, a youngish American, Washington Irving, was in England attending to the affairs of his firm. These went from bad to worse, and, as he was friendly with the English literary persons of his day, he earned money by writing in a slightly idealised manner about the British, so helping to build up something of a legend, if one that was founded on a good deal of fact, which had considerable influence on both sides of the Atlantic. He was, no doubt, one of those responsible for originating the fashion for the landscaping which has so largely prevailed in North America. He introduced this to his countrymen in the following terms: 'The taste of the English in the cultivation of land, and in what is called landscape-gardening, is unrivalled. They have studied nature intently, and discover an exquisite sense of her beautiful forms and harmonious combinations. Those charms, which in other countries she lavishes in wild solitudes, are here assembled round the haunts of domestic life. They seem to have caught her coy and furtive graces, and spread them, like witchery, about their rural abodes. Nothing can be more imposing than the magnificence of English park scenery. Vast lawns that extend like sheets of vivid green, with here and there clumps of gigantic trees, heaping up rich piles of foliage; the solemn pomp of groves and woodland glades, with the deer trooping in silent herds across them; the hare, bounding away

98 (*opposite*) The house and garden at Easthampton, Long Island, designed by Mary Deputy Cattell. The photograph was taken in early June

99 Mill Neck, Long Island, an American estate designed by Innocenti and Webel. The picture shows the outlet of a pond bordered by forget-me-nots and primroses

to the covert; or the pheasant, suddenly bursting upon the wing; the brook, taught to wind in natural meanderings, or expand into a glassy lake: the sequestered pool, reflecting the quivering trees, with the yellow leaf sleeping on its bosom, and the trout roaming fearlessly about its limpid waters, while some rustic temple or sylvan statue, grown green and dark with age, gives an air of classic sanctity to the seclusion.'

It is interesting to compare this with the comments of David Douglas, who had been sent in 1823, only a year or two later, by the Horticultural Society of London to study and collect in the eastern United States. 'Mr van Ralsen of Albany,' he wrote, 'has a large space of ground occupied as a pleasure or flower garden, which is a novelty in America, as little attention is paid to anything but what brings money or luxury for the table.' Rather more enterprising was Mr Jesse Bull, also of Albany. 'His garden is large and all divided by hedges of hawthorn from Britain. Hedging is a thing unknown in a general sense.' We must recall that though this might be the general picture of American gardening at that time, there were also notable pioneers. John Bartram had an immense correspondence and interchange of plants with Europe, founding his famed botanical garden near the Schuylkill River, then outside Philadelphia, in 1728; his son William, who was incidentally a talented botanical artist, carried on this work and did not die until the year that Douglas visited America. Thomas Jefferson, too, had a fine collection of plants in his garden at Monticello: in 1786 he visited most of the famous English landscape gardens, which he praised highly. Later, Andrew Downing of New York (1815-52) pioneered Repton's principles with great effect in his *Landscape Gardening* of 1841.

This linking of the introduction of *le jardin anglais* in North America in the early nineteenth century with David Douglas's visit is not done fortuitously here. For, as the grand manner of Le Nôtre reached those centres most remote from France just as it was collapsing under the influence of the English style, so the English manner reached America at a time when it had risen to its highest peaks and was about to descend. And strangely enough, David Douglas was one of those responsible. For in 1824 he made his second journey to the American continent, this time to the virtual *terra incognita* of the North Pacific coast. There he found and collected from a flora that would thrive in most temperate parts of the world, so rich a harvest that it brought about a new conception of gardening. Particularly important were the huge and fast-growing Pacific conifers [figure 100]. Except in a few instances—such as Endsleigh and Stourhead—existing gardens could not assimilate them: their planters did not as yet know their shapes and colours, and countless errors of taste resulted. At this period the science of horticulture was progressing fast, and many new plants were streaming into Europe from all parts of the world besides America. Repton's re-introduction of the formal flower garden was but the beginning of a fashion that ended with the annual bedding-out of tender exotics. Little more than a decade after Douglas's last journey, Robert Fortune made his first journey to China, from where he was to bring further riches and novelties. All these had somehow to be fitted into the garden.

And then there were other complications. In many countries the middle classes were prospering as they had never done before. Small villas sprang up in rows; their owners had little traditon to guide them. They were helped to achieve their successes by numerous devices provided for them by the march of science. Cast iron came to the help of structures; mass production became general and reduced costs. For the reviving fashion, often in a debased form, of the formal traditions of Italy and France, imitation stone fountains [figure 101], vases, columns and statues, all mass-produced and standardised, could be acquired cheaply. Particularly in these smaller gardens did the twining path,

100 The Araucaria at Dropmore, which in 1881 had attained a height of sixty-one feet

101 Detail of a fountain at Witley Court, Worcestershire, an extravagant Italianate garden of the late nineteenth century

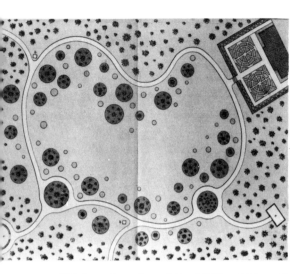

102 A garden-plan of the 1850's which well illustrates the transition from the classical layout (top right) to the meandering paths and scattered ornamental trees and shrubs of the Victorian age

often incongruously mingled with the classic manner [figure 102], resemble more than ever the meanders of an intoxicated man.

Those gardens that were designed in the grand manner were now faced with an incongruous mixture of styles from which to choose. And so, as at Alton, the abundantly wealthy sixteenth Earl of Shrewsbury, 'fond of architecture and gardening, but with much more fancy than judgement', in about 1814, began a huge undertaking to include something in every style, later known as Alton Towers [figure 103]. It was not untypical, though on a more grandiose scale, of many new developments that were undertaken in many parts of the world during the nineteenth century. An anonymous authoress at about the same period urged the planting of a 'mingled garden'—a general mixture of all kinds of plants. The Earl of Shrewsbury and those of his point of view acted on the same lines on a stupendous scale. The place stood—the gardens still remain—in the picturesque valley of the River Churnet in Staffordshire. The approach roads were then private and several miles long, passing through wild, rocky scenery. The first object that met the eye on entering the grounds was a Gothic bridge, reached by an embankment; no stream passed under it, but above it was a pond. Beyond this was a replica of the prehistoric monument, Stonehenge. Nearby was a range of seven conservatories with elegant glass domes, richly gilt. Beyond, on a bold, naked rock, was a lofty Gothic tower; at its base, an extraordinary cork-screw fountain—still to be seen. The rest of the valley, with more lakes, was filled with such objects as a Grecian temple, labyrinthine terraces, trellis-work, arbours, stone stairs, wooden stairs, turf stairs, gravel walks, turf walks, parterres, seats, flower-baskets, ivied walls, rock-work, shell-work, root-houses, moss-houses, and dead trees. A cottage for a blind harper as large as a farmhouse, and a mass of solid rock disguised to look like a thatched roof with dormer windows, were among the numerous other

103 Alton Towers, a fantastic English representation of a Chinese garden, made for the Earl of Shrewsbury

fantasies undertaken in all seriousness. Demonstrating the glories of progress was the Chinese pagoda fountain standing on an island. As much of it as was ever finished still remains. The base was of stone, the remainder of cast iron. Inside was a gasometer, which was to provide the light for the numerous dangling lanterns. The jet of water that was to emerge from this strange piece of chinoiserie was to have sprayed to a height of seventy to eighty feet. This strangeness and lack of congruity—true, usually on a lesser scale—was typical of nineteenth-century gardens. It was, almost everywhere, an age of ill-considered eclecticism.

The nineteenth-century garden, then, that surrounded a palace, a mansion, a large villa or a smaller suburban home —bearing in mind, of course, that the house itself might be in any style—was probably arranged something like this. Around the house there would be formal treatment, which was called in contemporary descriptions architectural or geometrical; this might or might not match the style of the house itself, and its detail might (or more probably would not) be scholarly and accurate. This would then lead on to the flower garden—an area of lawns, through which trimly-kept and usually narrow paths meandered in an undeterminate and usually aimless manner. In these lawns, if not already in the architectural area near the house, would be the parterres with their bedding-out. They would be framed with powdered mineral fillings—say of white

104 The Perseus fountain at Witley Court, Worcestershire, surrounded by a parterre in the Italian style

105 An avenue of Araucaria and Wellingtonia at Coombe Wood, 1880

spar, purple fluor-spar, grey-blue slate, red pounded brick and yellow pounded brick; the glitter of crushed coloured glass would be added. They would be filled with a rich variety of plants: scarlet and other pelargoniums, numerous kinds of verbena, tropaeolums in variety, calceolaris, and much else. The lawns would merge into dotted groups of shrubs and trees, planted in an irregular and usually rather spotty manner called gardenesque; variegated shrubs (gold and silver hollies, spotted ancubas) prevailed. In the larger gardens, this would then merge into the parkland, planted in the traditional picturesque manner, but now with a much wider choice of subjects. Possibly an added attraction would be a pinetum—a collection of conifers from many parts of the world. Here would be the strange *araucaria* [figure 105], said to defeat a monkey, and the giant *sequoia*. Not invariably were the quality of design and the workmanship poor. There were numerous exceptions. In 1848 Sir Charles Barry designed on little more than a shallow bank in the level countryside of Suffolk a huge Italian terraced garden at Shrubland Park for the rich Sir William Middleton. Down the centre falls a giant stairway in the manner of the Villa d'Este. The workmanship is fine—indeed, rather too much so, for it retains an over-mechanical appearance despite the passing of the years. Yet it must be acclaimed as a masterpiece of grandeur in garden architecture—of a rather peculiar kind, as is the strain of delight that it arouses. Another extravagant garden of this Italian type was also laid out by W. A. Nesfield at Witley Court, Worcestershire, for the Earl of Dudley rather later in the century [figure 104]. The cost was fantastic, as was the height to which the Perseus fountain threw its main jet, one hundred and twenty feet (the steam engine was a little more powerful than the devices employed at St Cloud.) More modest, and this time in Jacobean style, was the Hall at Bradford-on-Avon in Wiltshire [figure 106].

There is one feature of nineteenth century gardens that is, however, an invariable delight, being of a kind in which pomposity was impossible. That was the garden house. It took a great variety of forms. Sometimes, and most charmingly, it was the moss-house. Here a wooden-framed building was covered with a variety of mosses, held on by a pattern of slats, so as to form a living covering. Often the selection of the mosses was undertaken with great care to give variety to the surface and botanical interest. Another favourite was the root-house. In it the body of the building was formed of the gnarled bases and upper parts of the roots of tree trunks. The roof would most likely be thatched in a fanciful manner. Rustic-work summer arbours, Polish huts, Swiss chalets, Chinese 'kiosques', Indian seats and marquees were among other forms used for these little buildings, upon which more ingenuity was often lavished than upon more important buildings [figure 107].

So much artificiality, formality and incongruity was, quite apart from the now inevitable swings of fashion, bound to bring back the protean goddess of Nature in some form or another. She was on this occasion led by a combative Irish working gardener turned journalist, William Robinson. His campaign became really effective in 1872 when he first published his paper, *The Garden*. Shortly after, he met a talented artist and craftswoman, Miss Gertrude Jekyll, who was also interested in gardening; she, too, was a convincing writer. It is beyond doubt that these two, both great admirers of the later Reptonian stages of the English picturesque landscape garden, brought into being a new kind of gardening with a whole range of fresh garden delights.

106 The terrace of the Hall at Bradford-on-Avon, a nineteenth-century garden in the Jacobean style

107 An Indian garden-seat in cast-iron and sheet-copper

108 Gertrude Jekyll regarded the shapes, colours, foliage and growing habits of plants as important details to consider when planning a border

109 Daffodils planted thickly in a woodland garden, a method favoured by William Robinson

It was also a kind of gardening suited to small and large gardens alike, and well adapted to the twentieth century that was just round the corner. It is a style that, with little variation, is fundamental to countless modern gardens on both sides of the Atlantic. In it architecture plays only a minor part. But if there are fine buildings, terraces, fountains or ornaments already present they are not abolished. Instead, they are taken in as part of the scheme and suitably adorned with hardy, permanent plants. In the Robinsonian movement crude, elaborate parterres and bedding out are absolutely forbidden. Great emphasis is laid on colour schemes—working with the colours of flowers and plants to produce a considered design in colour. Very important are the plants themselves, their forms, habits and colours—not only of flower but foliage [figure 108]. Robinson and Miss Jekyll both had a profound knowledge of hardy plants, greater than their predecessors. (Here it should be mentioned that though Robinson in particular was most decided in his writings and intolerant of those who opposed him, in practice any really first-rate gardening met with his approval).

The great difference between the Robinsonian school and the earlier English landscape school is that it takes the lie of the land much more as it finds it, and then produces its effects by planting alone. William Robinson never worked from a drawn plan. He worked directly from the land and its features, whether they were trees, existing buildings, lakes or streams. In a grassy meadow, open woodland or an old orchard he would plant masses of daffodils, strewn as they would be in nature [figure 109]. His flower-beds were simple in shape and planted with variety. His paths would be wide and sensible, perhaps under a plain pergola. He had a personal aversion to the western American conifers—which did not stop others employing them most successfully in his style—but he was able to make use of the steadily increasing kinds of rhododendrons that were becom-

110 Killerton, Devon. One of the first English gardens to be planted as wild woodland

ing available. This shrub, where it can be grown, has played an important part in the modern garden; there were well-known and very delightful kinds grown in the late eighteenth and early nineteenth century, some from North America, but it was not until after J. D. Hooker's return from his journey in 1851 with seed of many Himalayan rhododendrons that the great possibilities of the Asiatic kinds with their variety of form, foliage, and flower became generally known. Soon, the hybridists were at work on them, and in the early part of the present century plant collectors, following in the footsteps of the botanical French Jesuit missionaries in Western China, brought hundreds of new kinds. They have become, as it were, the foundation shrubs of the twentieth-century woodland garden that developed from Robinson's idea of naturalising plants to form a wild garden. Many other shrubs suitable for this naturalising became available during the same period. Magnolias, forsythias, and a great variety of wild roses are now well known among them. In Britain, they were first grown and planted out to form an entirely new type of almost permanent wild woodland garden, improving as the years passed, by a handful of enthusiasts. Such were the Aclands at Killerton in Devon ; Arthur Soames of Sheffield Park in Sussex; J. C. Williams of Caerhays Castle in Cornwall; Osgood Mackenzie at Inverewe in Wester Ross, Scotland; and the Hon H. D. Maclaren (later Lord Aberconway) at Bodnant in North Wales [figure 111].

111 Bodnant, in north Wales, combines the formality of descending terraces with a large area of wood planted with flowering shrubs

112 The daffodil garden of Mrs Ricardo C. Gonzales, at Rye, New York, designed and planted by James S. Jack

A new manner of gardening had come into being. It was of woodland (and often water) in which exotic conifers, full of subtle variety in form, colour and texture, and ranging through every shade of green, were combined with deciduous trees that flower in many seasons of the year, and, having flowered, often shed their leaves in a blaze of glory. All these trees arise over a layer of shrubs that also scintillate with colour at their due times of the year. Among these, in turn, are naturalised woodland bulbs and herbs. Robinson's idea of the wild garden was the starting point of all this beauty, which has an added advantage and pleasure in that something similar can be made in the smallest copse, or even among a few fruit trees in an old orchard.

One of the pioneers in the collection of these trees and shrubs of the temperate climates was Charles Sprague Sargent, who founded the Arnold Arboretum near Boston,

Massachussetts, in 1872. Sargent was a great student of the rich flora of trees and shrubs in North America and an enthusiast for their cultivation in gardens as well as being a leading authority on those of Japan. It is not surprising, therefore, that many fine gardens in the new manner were made in America. These, on account of climatic conditions, are often rather similar to those of Europe [figure 112]. Down in the south, the climate is different. Here grow the magnolias (*M. grandiflora*, a huge evergreen tree which has long been famous in Europe, is one of them) and the ancient swamp cypresses among live (evergreen) oaks, dogwoods, and palmettos. The trees are draped with silvery Spanish moss. Under these conditions, many rhododendrons, camellias and azaleas from the Orient will thrive. Advantage has been taken of these circumstances to make some remarkable gardens. Two, the Middleton and Magnolia Gardens, are near Charleston [figure 116], whose plant-life is always associated with Dr Alexander Garden, the eighteenth-century botanist who explored it (and who incidentally gives his name to the Gardenia). On the Cooper River are the Cypress Gardens. Here from 1927 onwards, what was once a rice field was converted by the energies of Benjamin Kitteridge into a strange and original garden. Here, among the moss-draped *Taxodiums*, their gnarled breathing-knees, 'like some weird underwater defence system', alley-ways in the black water now lead past plantations of azaleas, daffodils, camellias and many other exotic plants, while in places the bines of flowering creepers climb the trees. The Magnolia Gardens, on the Ashley River [figure 116], are older. They were largely created by the Reverend John Grimké-Drayton, who died in 1891. One huge magnolia only now survives from the original avenue that gave the garden its name, though giant old plants of florist's azaleas and camellias remain.

An American garden designer who was in many ways the counterpart of Miss Jekyll was Mrs Beatrix (Max) Farrand (1873-1959). She had the same scholarly approach (her col-

113 The Huntington gardens at San Marino, California, among the most famous gardens in the United States. This is the main avenue bordered by statues

lection of gardening books of all countries and periods was given to the University of California) and had travelled widely to study her subject. A celebrated example of her work was, with Mrs Robert Woods Bliss, the creation of Dumbarton Oaks gardens around a house built in 1801 in Georgetown, Washington, DC. Here and elswhere she was able to work on a far greater scale than ever was vouchsafed to Miss Jekyll. Mrs Farrand visited England in 1933 to plan the layout of Dartington Hall, near Totnes, Devon.

The prodigious eclecticism typical of one aspect of the American manner is seen in the Longwood Gardens, again a twentieth-century creation by Pierre du Pont on the site of an old estate, between 1906 and his death in 1954. Not far from Philadelphia, it is noted for such features as the illuminated electrically-controlled fountains, and a reconstruction of a part of the Villa Gamberaia water-garden.

All this grandeur should not distract us from the smaller gardens around the old colonial-type houses [figure 98]. They have a long history and descent. The State of Georgia claims that its gardening record antedates that of any other state, for in 1566 the Spanish governor Menendez de Aviles established a settlement on an island south of the estuaries of the Savannah River called Santa Catalina, and here the monks no doubt practised horticulture as they did elsewhere. Later, in Savannah, James Oglethorpe established a botanical and horticultural garden for the benefit of the community as early as 1733.

Though Miss Gertrude Jekyll, but four years younger than William Robinson, was closely associated with him in her work, and is linked with him as the originator of a new type of garden, there can be little doubt that had she not met him, she would have continued her own distinctive manner of reformation. She was by training an artist and craftswoman; it was her upbringing and home life that had given her a profound knowledge of plants, and incidentally of the traditional craft connected with building. Her great contribution was the attention that she gave to colour in gardens. It is not insignificant that she was in her early years a successful designer of fabrics—she designed quite celebrated curtains for the Duke of Westminster at Eaton Hall in Cheshire. One thinks, therefore, of her celebrated herbaceous borders of hardy plants as being worked like a piece of subtly coloured embroidery; in them she added something quite new, and independent of William Robinson, to the pleasures of gardening. The same style of talent was devoted to her rose gardens. Instead of massed, regularly drilled beds, and rows of standards, she combined many kinds together, using both old ones long out of fashion and good new ones; she particularly delighted in skilfully draping climbing roses over aged walls and buildings.

Miss Jekyll's interest in the materials and craftsmanship of building has been mentioned. This led to a famous but very localised partnership with Sir Edwin Lutyens, perhaps the last architect to work in a style and with a feeling that was reminiscent of the Renaissance grand manner. She designed the planting of his formal gardens, which

114 Daneway in Gloucestershire represents all that is most individual in the small English garden today — lawn, yews, raised and herbaceous borders, and a background of mixed natural and planted trees — all blending perfectly with the Cotswold stone of the house

were of immense ingenuity, and displayed an ingenious use of traditional materials, with which he surrounded his houses. The number of Lutyens-Jekyll houses and gardens (even if we add those of their imitators) is relatively small. It is, however, largely attributable to their influence, supported by a band of scholarly architects equally devoted to the study of old buildings and the use of old materials, that a very great many, often quite small, old houses were made habitable under modern conditions and surrounded by gardens which though no slavish imitation of the past, were congruous with the buildings that they admirably displayed. This movement for the acquisition and restoration of houses, which were often, because they were alleged to be old-fashioned, going to rack and ruin, though of considerable architectural merit, seems to have started in England towards the end of the nineteenth century. It has, of course, been widely followed elsewhere.

Many examples could be mentioned. An excellent one that may be singled out, as it is an instance of Anglo-American co-operation, is Sulgrave Manor in Northamptonshire. Here we have a beautiful, small, grey-stone house of the sixteenth century, home of the ancestors of George Washington, that had declined into a farm house. It was restored to its original condition, and the gardens, keeping the old features such as a fine walnut tree, were made in a quiet and unobtrusive manner that well displays the house; yet no one could deny that much of the charm of the place is due to this sensitively designed garden.

There was at least one garden designer of the Robinsonian era who showed a true genius in incorporating a miscellany of works of art into a garden scene. Harold Peto was an architect who enjoyed working in the classical manner. He was a lover of pillars and porticos, terraces and fountains. He was also a collector and connoisseur of works of art, with unexceptionable taste—particularly of statuary and ornaments: he was an echo of the eighteenth-century

115 Iford Manor, a garden created by Harold Peto between 1899 and 1933. The broad terrace is terminated by an eighteenth-century garden-house, and bordered by statues collected by Peto on his travels

collectors who returned home from the Grand Tour with their prizes. Further, he was cosmopolitan; he did much work in the Alpes Maritimes, as well as for such sophisticated patrons as the Countess of Warwick at Easton Lodge, Essex, and at Buscot Park, Berkshire, and in Surrey and Yorkshire. Here was a designer, one would say, whose work was opposed in every way to the influential body of Robinson's supporters who criticised so strongly 'those who needlessly carry the dead lines of the builder into the garden, which, above every other artificial creation, should give us the sweetest fellowship with Nature'. Surprisingly, we find Peto's work given the greatest prominence and frequently illustrated by several writers of the Robinsonian school. The reason is without doubt that he had a great understanding of the use of plants, and particularly of the setting of trees. Further, he had great talent in merging his architecture smoothly and effectively into the natural landscape.

111

116 The Magnolia Gardens, Charleston, designed by the Reverend John Grimké-Drayton (1815-1891). Flaming azaleas are set against the dark stems of tropical trees

Nowhere are all these virtues better displayed than at Iford Manor, which he purchased in 1899, and continued to develop until his death in 1933 [figure 115]. The site itself was one of charm and great possibilities. A small steep-sided and entirely secluded valley carries the little River Frome where the counties of Wiltshire and Somerset join. Beside it stands the old stone manor house, near to an ancient bridge. The gardens lie upwards from the house (at many points one sees it from above) and rise into thick and aged woodland at the top, the main level being a long broad and pillar-margined terrace-way. At the west end near the house, this begins with a seat, adjoining a well-head adapted from a rare sculptured capital from Ravenna. It is terminated and closed at the east by a small garden house, native to Iford, of the early eighteenth century. A wide flagged path centres this hanging terrace, bordered by beds filled with a rich variety of plants. As one advances, to the left are the richly wooded heights (with many fine trees added) and to the right a view over the lower part of the gardens, largely treated informally, and then over to the native farm and woodland of the far side of the valley. Most remarkable, however, is the skilful placing along the terrace-way of statuary and a variety of other ornaments, all of high merit, collected by Peto on his travels. To detail further the elaborations on either side and beyond, would be mere cataloguing. Notable, however, is the stairway up from the lowest level, on which the house stands, to the terrace, flanked by a small water garden (the woodland on the hill is full of springs—used to supply a variety of ponds), and beyond the garden house, the cloisters which house more of the collection and provide a further range of vistas. The whole exemplifies the designer's axiom that a garden in which stone and plants combine in just proportion is the most satisfying.

117 Monet's *Le Bassin aux Nymphéas*, now in the National Gallery,
London, painted in 1900

CHAPTER SEVEN

Greenhouses and

118 Cactuses in a hothouse, 1873

Alpine Gardens

TWO REVOLUTIONARY DEVELOPMENTS in gardening, though they had their origins much earlier, belong to the nineteenth century. They were results of rapid improvements in horticultural technique and science, and the greater mobility of man due to the extraordinary developments of transport and a temporary opening to foreigners of countries from which they had for centuries been practically excluded—a state, unhappily, which no longer exists. Rather strangely, they concerned the cultivation of plants growing in extreme and opposite conditions: the floras of the humid tropics and the icy mountain tops.

The discovery that plants from a warm climate could be cultivated in a colder one, if they were given shelter at the appropriate cold season, is an old one. It was certainly known in the Rome of Pliny's time, where the orange was grown; this evergreen, and its cultivation in specially constructed orangeries, particularly during the seventeenth and eighteenth centuries, might well form a study on its own. Oranges were something of a rarity in France when they were introduced from there to England about 1550. A century later, orangeries in Le Nôtre's gardens were becoming famous. Soon palatial houses for sheltering this sun-loving exotic in the cool English climate had become a usual structure in all large gardens. About 1760 Sir William Chambers produced the orangery at Kew [figure 121], preferable as an architectural to a horticultural structure. Far into the north spread the cult: even in Poland, at Lazienki,

119 (*left*) The interior of a greenhouse, by Renoir

120 (*right*) Berkely Castle, Gloucestershire, rising massive and aged to guard the Severn valley

121 The Orangery at Kew Gardens, London, built by Sir William Chambers in about 1760 to house the plants then arriving from hotter climates

122 The Orangery at Lazienki, Warsaw, constructed by the Italian architect, Domenico Merlini, to the order of King Stanislaus Augustus about 1780

is found a temple built to honour the cult [figure 122]. Apart from sheltering tender plants in buildings during the cold season, it was discovered at some unknown but early period that many kinds needed no more than the shelter of a wall to keep them alive. Particularly was this so with fruit.

The choicer pears, apricots, nectarines and peaches could be grown far into northern Europe, given the protection of walls.

By the end of the eighteenth century, the greenhouse had become a building with most of its sides and roof of glass (the glass roof seems to have been an important innovation). The methods of heating remained either unsatisfactory, due to the production of heat by actual combustion within the house, with consequent violent changes in temperature and fouled air, or by other methods more ingenious than reliable. It seems that the much more stable method of heating by the natural circulation of hot water through pipes was first used by Bonnemain at the Jardin des Plantes in Paris about the time of the French Revolution. This method then seems to have been ignored for some twenty or more years until its general adoption, first in England. From about that time, 'the grand cause of the improvement of the design of hothouses may be traced to their design being no longer under the control of mansion architects'—an early instance of functionalism. Particularly good early examples of this new style of 'forcing garden' are shown in Humphry Repton's *Fragments of Landscape Gardening* of 1816. Among distinguished later examples were Joseph Paxton's Victoria House at Chatsworth of 1850, now destroyed. This was built to house the giant Amazonian water lily, known botanically as *Victoria amazonica*. The flowering in 1849 of this plant, with its floating leaves like six-foot wide tea-trays (large enough to carry little Miss Paxton dressed as a fairy) was in itself an achievement demonstrating the great increase in skill of gardeners and their new mastery of greenhouse management. Paxton's big new house led to many more even bigger. Another huge structure was the Jardin d'Hiver in Paris [figure 123], which had been built in the Champs Elysées in 1846, and looked 'at first sight, fairy land, so grand, lofty, tasteful, light and elegant does the whole appear'.

123 The *Jardin d'Hiver* in Paris, a huge structure which anticipated by a few years Joseph Paxton's more famous Crystal Palace

124 The Peterhof, Leningrad, begun by the French designer Le Blond for Peter the Great in 1716. The great canal, lined with fountains, leads from the palace towards the sea

125 (*right*) Sissinghurst Castle, Kent. A famous garden made by V. Sackville-West and Harold Nicolson among the rose-brick buildings of a Tudor house. The garden was not started until 1930, but already appears centuries old

126 A nineteenth-century print of the interior of a hothouse at Renwegg, containing 'foliage plants'

127 A partly artificial mossy grotto, a favourite nineteenth-century setting for plants

There were many other developments of the greenhouse in the late nineteenth century. There began a vogue for tender plants with brilliant and often bizarrely variegated foliage [figure 126]. The cults of such subjects as cinerarias, calceolarias, pelargoniums and tender primulas had their origins at this time; these and other greenhouse plants were soon developed almost out of recognition by the florists and hybridisers. Cactuses, those weirdly formed plants from the arid parts of the American continent [figure 118], and succulents such as mesembryanthemums from similar areas in South Africa, came into fashion. Orchard houses for growing fine fruit were introduced. Scientific research showed that careful control of soil rather than air temperature was the secret of growing superb pineapples, and pineries, with the soil-bed heated, were designed. As a result, in 1878 a pine named Lady Charlotte Rothschild was producing fruit of superlative quality weighing over nine pounds in weight.

The first non-scientific rock-gardens seem to have been largely connected with man's love of playing with stones and water (the child's delight in building sandcastles, or damming a gutter fast-flowing after a storm and then releasing the pent waters). Early nineteenth-century books describe this type of thing made from piles of rocks, tree-roots, clinkers and quartz. McIntosh in 1838 wrote of the making of a water-basin garden, around which wild plants were grown, to form a mossy grotto [figure 127], adding that if the water supply was connected to the hot water system of the house, half-hardy plants could be used. A few pioneers made intelligent attempts to create rock gardens in a natural manner. Sometimes these were quite incongruous imitations of a whole mountain on a midget scale, but William Wells had at the time of his death in 1836 completed a remarkable and pioneering example of a natural kind at Redleaf in Surrey [figure 128]. This type of garden remained most unusual for another fifty years or more, when a general trend towards rockeries constructed in

accordance with geology became the vogue. The York-shire firm of Backhouse led the way in this, and built many very well-designed and often large structures. The real surge of the cult of the rock garden, with which was often rather illogically combined a small water or bog garden, did not arrive until even later. Its high priests were such men as Henri Correvon in Switzerland and particularly Reginald Farrer in Britain. The influence of the latter, on account of his brilliant writing, was transcendental. It began with his book *My Rock Garden* of 1907, which resulted in every enthusiastic gardener making a rockery on his pattern, and was fortified by his great study, *The English Rock Garden* of 1919, and still shines brightly, long after his lonely death in 1920 on a plant-hunting expedition in 'the everlasting rain and mist' of Upper Burma. Farrer's methods, thanks perhaps to his glittering prose, were welcomed in North America. There is a fine example of the use of rock and water in a grand yet discreet manner at the New York Botanic Gardens [figure 131]. As a contrast, the intimacy of this kind of gardening and the beauty of effect attainable is seen in a smaller modern American garden [figure 130]. There is no doubt, as Sir Austen Chamberlain prophesied, that the pres-ent popularity of rock gardens is because they are ideally suited to amateurs with little time to spare, who can add

128 William Wells' rock-garden at Redleaf, Surrey, completed by 1836. This pioneering experiment was known as the 'rocky lawn', with a rock-walk in the foreground, a cedar and 'precipices' beyond

129 (*left*) Hidcote, Gloucestershire, an English garden created by an American, Lawrence Johnston

130 A corner of a contemporary garden at Fort Worth, Texas, designed
by Gene Schrickel Jr, and showing some Japanese influence

131 Primulas around a pond in the New York Botanic Gardens

interest to their enjoyment by spending their short vacations among the exhilarating mountains seeking the plants they grow. And then, too, a few square yards of garden can contain an exciting collection of the flora of the Alps, well secreted from prying eyes. This fact was pointed out as long ago as 1830 by a certain Thomas Miller of St Clairtown in Scotland who built himself a rockery on a small plot quite surrounded with houses, yet ingeniously concealed from them so that he might feel he was enjoying the noble solitude of the peaks.

Latterly, Nature has been inclined to slip out of the alpine garden. The aesthetic uses of rocks and rock plants (perhaps from Japanese influence) has tended to come to the fore, the plantsman having to take second place. Possibly in retaliation he has begun to cultivate his more unwilling pets in pots and pans in scientifically designed glasshouses, or in cunningly devised soil mixtures formed into 'table-top' beds. It must be admitted that gems from the high Alps seem often to prefer these methods and thrive better than in imitations of their natural surroundings.

We have called one section of this book 'Nineteenth-Century Variety'. Where, then, does the Twentieth come in? It will be seen that it is difficult to divide them. The gardens of the first part of the twentieth were in a manner that developed in the late part of the nineteenth: both had their roots in the gardens of the late eighteenth and very first years of the nineteenth—a leap back to the Reptonian vision over a large part of the intervening years. Even today, when we are more than half through the twentieth century, it seems that most garden designers still look back to that period for their inspiration—or even, as at Hidcote Manor in the Cotswolds [figure 129], range further into the past. Lawrence Johnstone took hints from many periods and countries and composed them into a charming unity. Particularly had he an understanding of space and a masterly power of handling horticultural material. Side by side, always ingeniously linked, lie a long formal vista and a wild garden meandering round a stream. Few gardens summarise so extensively, if sometimes in the tiniest way, the gamut of garden pleasures (including the unusual one of wit) and include among its plants so many treasures.

Now we must look keenly at the present as it leads to the future; we must seek its essential qualities. And it is not difficult to find them: dense, sky-reaching urbanism and the escape therefrom, to suburbanism and the world of the commuter. Of the first, we may look at the American sky-scraper garden, of straightforward design, belonging to Baron Waldemar von Zedtwitz [figure 132]. Or we can examine the little city patio garden of a house in East 81st Street, New York, formed of well unified assemblage of features that are quite original yet evocative of other styles [figure 133].

Of gardens in the outer world centering on cities, it is more difficult to find satisfying instances. To find a distinctive period style that is neither conventional nor abounding in 'contemporary' architectural clichés is not easy. Surely, to

132 A pent-house garden in New York belonging to Baron Waldemar von Zedtwitz

133 The patio garden at the rear of a house at East 81st Street, New York City, designed by Lloyd Bell

134 A forcing-garden in winter, 1816

carry out a formal layout based on a geometrical abstract painting or to plan flower-beds in the amorphous shapes of a Klee whimsicality, is scarcely true design executed with conviction. Perhaps the signposts are to be found in some Scandinavian countries, or in the high imagination shown in a contemporary garden at Fort Worth, Texas, with its faint echoes of Japan [figure 130]. For the time being, the least we can do is to try and maintain the steadily decreasing numbers of great gardens of the past as well as may be possible.